Death doesn't exist

The Mother on Death
Sri Aurobindo on Rebirth

Impressum

Acknowledgments: It took millennia to evolve from animal to man; today man, thanks to his mind, can accelerate things and will a transformation towards a man who will be God. This transformation with the help of the mind, through self-analysis, is a first stage; afterwards, vital impulses must be transformed - which is far more difficult; then, most of all, the physical: each cell of our body will have to become conscious. It is the work I am doing here. It will allow the conquest of death. It's another story; that will be future mankind, perhaps in centuries, perhaps sooner. It will depend on men, on peoples. Auroville is the first step towards this goal.

Mother's Agenda, 28.2.68 All texts are the copyright of the Sri Aurobindo Ashram Trust Pondicherry

First Edition 2015
Second Edition 2022
Death doesn't exist
Prisma

ISBN 978-93-95460-00-2 (print)
ISBN 978-93-95460-01-9 (ebook)

BISAC Code:
SEL010000, SELF-HELP / Death, Grief, Bereavement
PHI034000, PHILOSOPHY / Social
PHI015000, PHILOSOPHY / Mind & Body

Thema Subject Category:
FXL, Narrative theme: Death, grief, loss
QRVK, Spirituality and religious experience

Cataloging-in-Publication Data for this title is available from the Library
of Congress.

Printed and bound in India by:
PRISMA, Aurelec/ Prayogshala,
Auroville 605101, Tamil Nadu, India

Digital Editions produced by:
DMI Systems Pvt Ltd, Vishnupuri,
Aligarh 202001, Uttar Pradesh, India

Published by PRISMA, an imprint of Digital Media Initiatives
www.prisma.haus, www.dmi.systems

Although Death walks beside us on Life's road,

A dim bystander at the body's start

And a last judgment on man's futile works,

Other is the riddle of its ambiguous face:

Death is a stair, a door, a stumbling stride

The soul must take to cross from birth to birth,

A grey defeat pregnant with victory,

A whip to lash us towards our deathless state.

Savitri, Book X, The Book of the Double Twilight, Canto 1
The Dream Twilight of the Ideal, p.600

Contents

Fear of the dead

Why death happens?

The consciousness at the time of death

Preface

Death is a continuous challenge to human beings. It hovers as a threat over man's head, as at any time the fateful moment can arrive. The quest for immortality has therefore always been a major spur to man's creative aspiration, be it in arts, literature, politics or warfare. To gain immortal fame as an artist, a writer, a statesman or a conqueror, to engrave one's memory in the annals of fate, has always been and still is a tremendous motivation for mankind.

But all these exploits are confined to the realm of transcience. Fame may remain, works stay for millennia at the best, but the person as such is gone. The highest form so far to fulfill this aspiration has therefore been the quest for immortality of the person, lifting him above the destroying roar of the waters of time.

In its usual form this immortality has been connected to the soul, the psychic being, the Atman. This quest for immortality has been the motive force behind the aspiration of the rishis, it made the ancients mummify the bodies of the deceased, it inspired religions promising eternal life to the believers.

The Death of Death is also one of the promises of Sri Aurobindo's and Mother's yoga. But it goes much farther: even physical immortality is proposed, something which had never been realized before. To look into this quest as expressed in 'Mother's Agenda' and to try to understand the conditions of its fulfilment is the subject of this compilation.

First we will look at the nature of death as explained by the Mother, next we examine the conditions which bring death and those who are believed to make the conquest of death possible. Finally we will take a glance at Mother's own experiences with death, her preparatory work for the final victory.

1906, Tlemcen, Algeria

Note on the Mother

The Mother was born Mirra Alfassa on February 21st, 1878, in Paris. A student at the Academie Julian, she became an accomplished artist. Gifted from an early age with a capacity for spiritual and occult experience, she went to Tlemcen, Algeria, in 1906 and 1907 to study occultism with the adept Max Théon and his wife.

Between 1911 and 1913 she gave a number of talks to various groups of seekers in Paris and began to record her deepening communion with the Divine in the diary later published as Prayers and Meditations.

In 1914 the Mother voyaged to Pondicherry, South India, to meet the Indian mystic Sri Aurobindo. After a stay of eleven months, she was obliged by the outbreak of the First World War to return to France. A year later she went to Japan, where she remained for four years.

In 1920 the Mother rejoined Sri Aurobindo in Pondicherry. Six years later, when the Sri Aurobindo Ashram was founded, Sri Aurobindo entrusted its material and spiritual charge to her, for he considered her not a disciple but his spiritual equal and collaborator. Under her guidance the Ashram grew into a large, many-faceted spiritual community.

She also established a school, the Sri Aurobindo International Centre of Education, in 1952, and the international township of Auroville in 1968.

Her teachings have been published in the Collected Works of the Mother, which to date comprise 17 volumes. Additionally, in Mother's Agenda, a 13-volume record of her conversations with her disciple Satprem, the Mother also gave a detailed account of her exploration into the body-consciousness, and her discovery of a "cellular mind" capable of restructuring the nature of the body and the laws of the species.

The Mother passed away on November 17th, 1973.

Pathways for the Dead

*So many people come to her in the night for the passage to the
other side whom she has not known in the body.*

– Sri Aurobindo

Even before Mirra discovered the teaching of the Cosmic
Movement, she had 'certain experiences at night, certain types
of nightly activities, caring for people who had just left their
body.' Although still lacking the theoretical knowledge, she
knew exactly what had to be done, and did it. When she began
reading the *Revue Cosmique*, she understood many things she
had not known before and, true to character, began to apply
that new knowledge and to work it out systematically.

'Every night at the same hour, my work consisted in
constructing between the purely terrestrial atmosphere and the
psychic atmosphere a sort of path of protection across the
vital, so that people wouldn't have to pass through it. For those
who are conscious but don't have the knowledge it's a very
difficult passage, it's infernal. I was preparing this path - it
must have been around 1903 or 1904, I don't exactly remember
- and working at it for months and months.' Afterwards, she
would be told by Madame Théon, with whom we shall soon
get acquainted: 'It is part of the work you have come on Earth
to do. All those with even a slightly awakened psychic being
and who can see your Light will go to it at the moment of
dying, wherever they may die, and you will help them to pass
through.' And the Mother said later that this was a 'constant
work' she had been doing and continued to do.

"And this is a constant work. Constant. It has given me a
considerable number of experiences concerning what happens
to people when they leave their bodies. I've had all sorts of
experiences all kinds of examples. It's really very interesting."

But something left her puzzled. "I have had all sorts of
experiences" Mother said, "for so many, so many years. For
about sixty years, constantly I have aided people who are said
to 'die'. Constantly. Well, there are almost as many cases as

there are people. At least twice it happened to me - in this very existence - 'to die', as people call it; and both times the experience was different, although the apparent fact was the same. What I was asking myself today is: Would what is called 'death' be, by chance, a multitude of different things?"

The human being consists of several sheaths or 'bodies', mental, vital and material, and behind them the soul, supporting the whole.[1] At the time of death, the incarnated soul lays down the material body and enters the vital worlds, through which it passes into the mental worlds, and finally into the psychic[2] world, where it rests 'in a kind of beatific contemplation' between two incarnations and assimilates its experiences in the former life. The beings of the vital worlds, more specifically the lower vital worlds, are the vicious entities we call demons or hostile forces. As these worlds are the first the departing soul has to traverse, it must in almost all cases confront those beings unprepared, unarmed with the necessary knowledge. It is on those terrifying experiences that the various myths of 'hell' have been based.

The Mother explained: 'Generally, one calls the "domain of death" a certain region of the most material vital into which one is projected at the moment one leaves the body.' This lower vital region, this material vital world, is obscure and full of small, vampire-like beings who feed on everything they can swallow, including the vital substance of the deceased person who, because of the sudden and often shocking death experience, has been projected into it. In the physical these beings are powerless, but when one has passed completely outside the physical - and the main characteristic of death is

---

1 This mental, vital and material 'whole' is called the adhara in Sanskrit. As this is a useful term which has no equivalent in English, it will be used in the rest of the book.

2 In this book the words 'psyche' (i.e. soul) and its derivations are used in the literal sense, as the Mother and Sri Aurobindo used them, and not as relating to occult or supernatural phenomena - except when otherwise stated.

that it cuts all links with the material world - one is at their mercy. 'If at that moment people who love the departed person concentrate their thought and love on him, he finds a refuge therein and this protects him fully against those entities.' One who does not have such protection is 'like a prey delivered to those forces, and that indeed is an experience that is difficult to bear.' It is 'infernal'.

And the Mother went on: 'Now there are what one might call bridges, protected passages which have been built in the vital world in order to pass through all those dangers. There are "atmospheres" which receive people leaving their body, give them shelter, give them protection.' These 'protected passages' are the ones she built for months on end somewhere at the beginning of the century. We now know from people who have actually died, but who for some reason or another have come back from death to go on living, that these bridges are there. These people are the ones who have had a 'near-death experience'.

Many books have already been published on the subject, which has been pioneered by Elizabeth Kübler-Ross and Raymond Moody. Let's take the one written by Peter and Elizabeth Fenwick, The Truth in the Light. A frequent scenario of the near-death experiences examined in the work is as follows: at the moment of death the experiencers have no fear at all. On the contrary, everything feels like a pleasant experience and even a great happiness. Many see themselves outside their (material) body. In a flash their past actions are reviewed tactfully and with a sense of humour, and then they enter a tunnel and are attracted by a warm, loving light; in that light, they discern a Being of Light, waiting to take them onwards. All this is accompanied with a 'mystical' feeling of intense realness, unity and ineffability of the experience. 'Sometimes the passage to the light that people describe is not really a tunnel, though it usually has tunnel-like features - and nearly always the welcoming light is seen shining more brightly at the end - at the end of 'protected passages'.

What is the difference between a death in the Ashram and a death outside? Does one get more benefit in the form of development of the mental, vital, etc, on their own planes so that one may get a better new birth?

I am not aware of any "development" of the mental, etc, in their planes; the development takes place on earth. The mental and other planes are not evolutionary.

The one who dies here is assisted in his passage to the psychic world and helped in his future evolution towards the Divine.

- Sri Aurobindo, 14th December 1936

The Mother, The Story of Her Life, Explorations of the Occult,
Georges Van Vrekhem, Harper Collins.

Bridge across the Afterlife[1]

In 1961 the Mother spoke in a private conversation about a certain activity of hers, begun when she was in her early twenties and continued since then without interruption. "It must be part of the work for which I have come on the Earth. For even before meeting Théon (her temporary teacher in occultism and the Kabbalah), before having any knowledge, I had experiences during the night, experiences of certain activities during the night in which I looked after people who were leaving their body. And I did that with a knowledge! - although I did not know anything, and neither did I try to know anything, or whatever. I knew exactly what had to be done, and I did it. I was about twenty at the time.

"As soon as I discovered the teaching of Théon, even before I met him in person, as soon as I read him and came to understand all kinds of things which I did not know before, I started working quite systematically. Every night at the same time I performed a work which consisted in constructing, between the purely terrestrial atmosphere and the psychic atmosphere, a *sort of protective pathways through the vital,* so that the people (who had just left their material body) would not have to traverse it any more. Because, for those who are conscient but do not have the knowledge, that is really very difficult: it is infernal." (It is precisely this knowledge which was provided in the Egyptian and Tibetan "books of the dead".) "It is infernal. So I built that. That was perhaps in 1902-1903 or 1904, I do not remember exactly. But month after month after month I worked at it.

"Afterwards, when I went to Tlemcen, I told all that to madame Théon. She said: 'Yes, this is part of the work you have come to do on Earth. All those whose psychic being is a little bit awake, and who are able to perceive your Light, will

---

1 This talk was given in Savitri Bhavan at Auroville, on 18th November 2010, in commemoration of the Mother's passing on 17th November 1973 by Georges Van Vrekhem.

go to your Light at the moment of death, wherever they may die, and you will help them cross beyond.' And that is a constant work.[2] Madame Théon was an even greater occultist than her husband." The Mother went two times to Tlemcen, in Algeria, in 1906 and 1907.

The "pathways" the Mother built are what is described by many persons who have been clinically dead as tunnels, bridges or narrow mountain passes by which they feel protected and which they use to cross over directly into the Light. They are able to report this kind of experience because, after having been clinically dead, they came back to life. Although the first reports date from the Second World War, "near-death experiences" started drawing the interest of the general public because of the 1975 book *Life After Life* by Raymond Moody, a medical doctor. According to a later Gallup poll no less than 8 million Americans claim to have had a near-death experience. Students of the phenomenon claim that the number of near-death experiences may be much higher, as many persons who have gone through the experience are reluctant to talk about it for fear of ridicule.

The *Britannica Concise Encyclopedia* defines "near-death experience" as follows: "Mystical or transcendent experience reported by people who have been on the threshold of death. The near-death experience varies with each individual, but characteristics frequently include hearing oneself declared dead, feelings of peacefulness, the sense of leaving one's body, the sense of moving through a dark tunnel toward a bright light, a life review, the crossing of a border, and meetings with other spiritual beings, often deceased friends and relatives. Near-death experiences are reported by about one-third of those who come close to death. Cultural and physiological explanations have been offered, but the causes remain uncertain. Typical after-effects include greater spirituality and decreased fear of death."

---

2 *L'Agenda de Mère,* vol. II, pp. 258-259.

As this definition indicates, "the near-death experience varies with each individual." Yet Elisabeth Kübler-Ross, "after listening to thousands and thousands of people," found that there are four successive main phases.[3]

1. People float out of their bodies; they are totally aware of the scene he or she has left and assume an ethereal shape; they experience wholeness.

2. They are able to go anywhere with the speed of thought; they meet their guardian angels or guides who comfort them with love and introduce them to the presence of previously deceased dear ones.

3. Guided by their guardian angel they enter what is commonly described as a tunnel, bridge or mountain pass; at the end they see a bright light which some call God; everybody agrees on one thing: that they were enveloped by overwhelming love, the purest of love. None wants to return to his or her physical body. All lives are changed after the experience.

4. They are in the presence of the Highest Source some call God; they no longer need their ethereal shape for they become spiritual energy; they experience a oneness, a completeness of existence. Some remember going through a life review, a process in which they confronted the totality of their life; they were made to understand the reason for every decision, thought and action they had in life.

It will surprise nobody that this subject, however well documented and confirmed by reliable persons, is the target of doubt and ridicule by scientific and other positivist-minded people. They object, for instance, that the immaterial is in principle unseen, unheard, and unable to be sensed or measured empirically, and therefore unprovable. Then they use anything, positivist or not, that might explain those experiences, including dreams arising from Carl Jung's collective unconscious; recollections of the birth experience, "an explanation proposed by the late Carl Sagan" (who was a cosmologist calling himself an "exobiologist"); the effects of

____

3 Elisabeth Kübler-Ross: *The Wheel of Life*, pp.195

drugs and medicines; carbon dioxide intoxication or oxygen starvation; or a flood of endorphins released by the dying brain, etc.

Obviously, this flood of experiences exceeds the boundaries of physical science, which by now at least should be used to the astonishing and apparently impossible in its own backyard. Only the science of yoga, and its experiential knowledge of reality and the human personality can explain them.

A human being consists of more than a body, and even more than a body-plus-mind as has been the belief in the West since its classical times. To this body-plus-mind may be added a soul, although the Western philosophers and theologians have generally identified the soul with the mind, both being "non-material". According to the common yogic experience, however, a human being consists of several bodies or sheaths, material, vital, and mental, contained in each other. At the centre of this complex being sits the soul or psychic being, which has taken up its bodies in reverse order when descending into a new terrestrial incarnation.

The material body is the one that dies, while the vital and mental bodies survive for some time, still enveloping the soul. It is in this condition that everyone has to traverse the worlds that correspond to the state of his vital body and the development of his mental body. In most cultures and individual cases the mental body does not possess the necessary knowledge to protect the transiting person. The lower regions of the vital plane can be, as the Mother said, "infernal" or hellish, inhabited by hellish beings. (The concept of hell originated from the remembrance of this kind of post mortem experiences.) The Mother constructed the "protective pathways" precisely to protect the deceased against such hellish experiences and to have them transit directly to the plane of the psychic, which is a divine plane.

These protecting pathways are what gives the impression of a tunnel, a bridge, or a narrow mountain pass. Still carried by his vital and mental body sheaths, the transiting person perceives the Light of the higher, spiritual hemisphere (in fact the Mother's Light). The more he comes nearer to it, the more intense it becomes. As Kübler-Ross writes, that light "radiates intense warmth, energy, spirit and love - love most of all, unconditional love; they feel peace, tranquility and the anticipation of finally going home." The experiencers who have gone that far do not want to return to the dark, difficult and painful world which they have left behind; they want to discard their vital and mental sheaths too and enter there where all is existence, consciousness and bliss: the psychic world.

Knowledge physical and spiritual, and its seasons
If one had read earlier about the Mother's protective pathways across the afterlife, say before the publication of the first books on NDE, her narrative of what she had accomplished in the beginning of the 20th century might have looked like another of those chimerical experiences mystics think they have. Yet this is only one of many elements in Sri Aurobindo and the Mother's writings which have in the meantime come within the compass of science, and there will no doubt be more to come. For there is a spiritual knowledge which is independent of and more true than scientific materialism, bound by the limitations of the human mind. Spiritual insight is based on direct knowledge; mental activity remains inexorably restricted by the human constitution, as has been recognized by philosophers like Plato, Berkeley and Kant.

Another example of Sri Aurobindo and the Mother's "foreknowledge" is the very special nature and purpose of the Earth, as commented upon in the talk in 1956 and "2012: Doomsday?" It must suffice here to remind one that the Mother said in the 1950s: "From the occult and spiritual point of view, the Earth is the concentrated symbol of the universe. For the convenience and necessity of the work, the whole universe has been concentrated and condensed symbolically in a grain of sand which is called the Earth. And therefore it is the symbol of all - all that is to be changed, all that is to be transformed, all that is to be converted is here." At the time she said this, this sort of view was still squarely contradicted by the Copernican Principle[4], stressing the fact that the Earth was but one planet among possibly billions in the universe, and man no more than an animal among animals. Now, however, when indeed many "exoplanets" are discovered, this certainty is called into question in scientifically argued books like *Rare Earth* by Peter Ward and Donald Brownlee, *The Eerie Silence* and *The Goldilocks Enigma* by Paul Davies, and *The Privileged Planet* by Guillermo Gonzalez and Jay Richards.

The direct and continuous influence of the mind on the body has time and again been highlighted by Sri Aurobindo and the Mother, especially in matters of health and the doctor-patient relationship. At the centre of this topic are the power of a doctor's suggestions and the placebo effect. In a special file about the intriguing placebo effect and titled "When the spirit cures the body" the French science magazine *Sciences et Avenir* writes: "This powerful effect has been used since the night of time in the doctor-patient relationship, but without knowing its intimate secrets. Having remained obscure for a long time, it begins to be decrypted by a new discipline called neuro-endocrino-immunology, the study of the interactions between three principal systems of our organism. ... The placebo effect does exist!"[5]

The Mother has explained several times that the brain has the capacity to continue developing during its whole lifetime. Science, on the contrary, held that the enormous mass of neurons of this most complicated of objects in the universe was fixed once and for all, and that it could only diminish and degenerate. Recently this physiological tenet has been modified drastically. One reads now about the five ages of the brain and the fact that it continues evolving, even in advanced age, on condition that one does not stop stimulating it, in other words that one remains mentally active - or, as the Mother said, that one remains "young".

---

4 See talk 6: "Being Human and the Copernican Principle".

5 *Sciences et Avenir*, November 2005, p.62.

In one of the first chapters of *The Life Divine*, Sri Aurobindo wrote: "For it will be evident that essential Matter is a thing non-existent to the senses and only ... a conceptual form of substance, and in fact the point is increasingly reached where only an arbitrary distinction in thought divides form of substance from form of energy."[6] Now you find popular science books with a title such as *The Matter Myth*, and physicists who say: "Speaking as a physicist, I judge matter to be an imprecise and rather old-fashioned concept. Roughly speaking, matter is the way particles behave when a large number of them are lumped together. Matter is weird stuff..." (Freeman Dyson)[7] Or: "Quantum field theory paints a picture in which solid matter dissolves away, to be replaced by weird excitations and vibrations of invisible field energy. In this theory, little distinction remains between material substance and apparently empty space, which itself seethes with ephemeral quantum activity. ... Quantum physics undermines materialism because it reveals that matter has far less 'substance' than we might believe. ... Even the apparent solidity of ordinary matter melts away into a frolic of insubstantial patterns of energy."[8]

Already during the First World War, when writing the instalments that would become *The Life Divine*, Sri Aurobindo's interpretation of the terrestrial evolution contained elements which would only later enter the scientific discussion about the development of the life-forms. In those texts from the *Arya* we find what Eldredge and Gould would call "punctuated equilibrium" in 1972; the discussion of life in plants and a rather developed mind in higher animals; the statement that species, including the human, cannot evolve beyond themselves by their own effort; the confirmation that there have existed civilizations of which no trace is found today, and that peoples considered primitive a century ago

---

6 *Id.,* p.18.

7 Freeman Dyson: *Infinite in all Directions*, p.8.

8 Paul Davies and John Gribbin: *The Matter Myth*, pp.8 and 229.

were actually retrograde populations from former times; the standpoint that in evolution there is a design, defined by an intelligence and worked out by it, etc. And all this ordered within a coherent system, valid before the positivist theories of evolution (Lamarck, Darwin, de Vries, Neo-Darwinism) were fashioned, and equally valid after those theories have been seriously questioned and will - within a not too distant future - become history.

Remembering the Mother

Returning to our main theme, one could ask the question: Why was this invaluable protection after death provided only recently, so late in the history of our species?

An answer on this level of things is not to be given by mental understanding. As madame Théon told the Mother, building the bridges across the afterlife was part of what the Mother had come to do on Earth, and the light mentioned in all NDE experiences is the Mother's Light. In the words of madame Théon: "All those whose psychic being is a little bit awake, and who are able to perceive your Light, will go to your Light at the moment of death, wherever they may die, and you will help them cross beyond."

These words refer directly to the status of Mirra Alfassa, the French woman whom we now call "The Mother", thereby meaning the Great Mother incarnated as the female part of the Avatar Sri Aurobindo-Mother. Before, the Avatar had always been male, and many Hindus still have difficulty in accepting a male-female Avatar. But it is quite clear that if there is an earthly evolution, in which the successive Avatars play a crucial role, and if in the present stage of humanity's history this evolution is reaching a critical point, the Avatar has to represent in himself the complete human being in order to transfigure it. Only the Great Mother, because she manifests all levels of existence and also transcends them, could perform a task like building bridges across the planes of existence, and constantly help the dying onward to their psychic resting place.

The significance of "she whom we call the Mother" can

only be fully understood in her three aspects as the Great Mother of many names, but always "the one original transcendent Shakti"; as Mahashakti, the cosmic Mother of the Gods; and as the incarnated Mother in the Yoga.

The Great Mother is known in all great spiritual and occult traditions, even though variously named and described. We find her in Isis, Cybele, Sophia, and the Virgin Mary. She is the One who became Two - the active Brahman from eternity divided into Ishwara and Shakti, Purusha and Prakriti. On the *Origin of the World,* a gnostic text from around 200 CE, defines her in terms which, if properly understood, agree with those of the Vedantic scriptures:

It is I who am the offspring of what gave birth to me
(what gave birth to her being the One);
And it is I who am the Mother
(the Great Mother, the one original transcendent Shakti);
It is I who am the wife
(Shakti to Ishwara, in human metaphorical language);
It is I who am the virgin
(for ever the untouchable Origin of all);
It is I who am pregnant
(with all the power and manifestations of the universe);
It is I who am the midwife
*(the middle term chit-tapas in the Vedantic sat-chit/
tapasananda);*
It is I who am the one that comforts pains of travail
(who justifies the pains of the evolutionary manifestation);
It is my husband who bore me
(Ishwara is also the Brahman);
And it is I who am his mother
(who gives shape to him in his manifestation - Isis, Mary);
And it is he who is my father and my lord.
It is he who is my force
(because I am his force, Shakti);

I am in the process of becoming
(the complete Divine is growing up in the Manifestation),
Yet I have borne a Man as lord.
(the cosmic Purusha, the archetype of what humanity is to become).

The Mother herself gave us a glimpse of Mahashakti, the cosmic Mother, when she narrated one of her experiences on 3rd February 1958. "The Supramental world exists permanently and I am there permanently in a Supramental body. I had proof of it this very day, when my earth consciousness went there and remained there consciously between two and three o'clock in the afternoon. Now I know that what was lacking for the two worlds to join in a constant and consciousness relation is an intermediate zone between the physical world as it is and the Supramental world as it is..." She saw this intermediate zone as "a huge ship, as large as a city, which was a symbolic representation of the place where this work is going on." On board this ship were people "destined to become the future inhabitants of the Supramental world. They were trained for their task and ready to go ashore."

The Mother was in charge of the whole enterprise from the beginning and throughout the proceedings. "I had prepared all the groups myself. I stood on the ship at the head of the gangway, calling the groups one by one and sending them ashore."

During this experience the Mother was suddenly interrupted and called back into her physical body by somebody in her room, and had at that instant a brief glimpse of herself. "My upper part, particularly the head, was not much more than a silhouette of which the contents were white with an orange fringe. The more down towards the feet, the more the colour looked like that of the people on the ship, that is to say orange; the more upwards, the more it was translucent and white, with less red. The head was only a contour with a brilliant sun in it. Rays of light radiated from it, which were actions of the will."

And then there is "the Mother in the Yoga" who this time had not come as a *Vibhuti* (Hatshepsut, Jeanne d'Arc, Elisabeth[9]) but as the Avatar. Many devotees have difficulty in understanding the three aspects of the Mother, as she said herself. Most of them expect her to be shiningly divine in all her earthly ways, twenty-four hours a day. And that she was, of course, but not like the temple Gods or the Gods in the *Puranas.* For she was here not only in a human body, she had also to take upon her or rather into her the full human condition in order to transform it, more specifically the human condition of the disciples. To be a real guru is a task of which the disciples usually have no idea, for it means taking their shortcomings, deformations and subconscious darknesses upon oneself. Being the Avatar of the age meant not only that; it meant also having to suffer and transform all that was low and animal-like below and preceding the human condition.

One reads from the pen of several authors that "the Mother was so human." M.P.Pandit for instance wrote: "She was supremely divine but equally extremely human." This is a misconception of the Mother which interprets her perceptible actions and her gracious relations with people according to the human ways. Indeed, she had to move among the disciples, the Ashram youth and the visitors; she had to answer all kinds of questions instantly; she had to make decisions constantly; and she had to respond immediately to requests, prayers and inner expressions of adoration and love, but also to attitudes of anger, malevolence and even hate. Yet it was she who said: "It has come to the point that even those who are here put on me feelings and reactions which are purely human." In *Savitri* Sri Aurobindo wrote: "Even when she bent to meet earth's intimacies / Her spirit kept the stature of the Gods."

Some still consider the Mother to have been a disciple of Sri Aurobindo. It is therefore important to state that such was *not* the case. Sri Aurobindo had his amanuensis, Nirodbaran, write

____

9 See Georges Van Vrekhem: The *Mother — The Story of Her Life,* chapter 14.

to Arindam Basu: "The Mother is not a disciple of Sri Aurobindo. She has had the same realization and experience as myself." And he wrote in a letter: "What is known as Sri Aurobindo's Yoga is the joint creation of Sri Aurobindo and the Mother."[10] The equivalence of Sri Aurobindo and the Mother is evident when considering the following basic declarations. Sri Aurobindo: "The Mother's consciousness and mine are the same, the one Divine Consciousness in two, because that is necessary for the play." The Mother: "Without him I exist not, without me he is not manifest." These pronouncements reflect the truth of the Divine essence and its manifestation. "There is no difference between the Mother's path and mine," wrote Sri Aurobindo, "we have and have always had the same path, the path that leads to the Supramental change and the divine realization; not only at the end, but from the beginning they have been the same."[11]

The Mother herself narrates, in *Words of Long Ago*, how in 1912 she had noted down "the whole programme of what Sri Aurobindo has done and the method of doing the work on Earth. ... I met Sri Aurobindo for the first time in 1914, two years later, and I had already made the whole programme." That programme reads as follows: "The general aim to be attained is the advent of a progressive universal harmony. The means for attaining this aim, in regard to the Earth, is the realization of human unity through the awakening in all and the manifestation by all of the inner Divinity which is One. In other words: to create unity by founding the Kingdom of God which is within us all.

"The following is therefore the most useful work to be done: 1. For each individually, to be conscious in himself of the Divine Presence and to identify himself with it. 2. To individualize the states of being that till now were never conscious in man and thus to put the Earth in connection with one or more of the fountains of the universal force that are still

---

10 Sri Aurobindo: *On Himself,* p.459.
11 *Ibid., p.459.*

sealed to it. 3. To speak again to the world the eternal word under a new form adapted to its present mentality it will be the synthesis of all human knowledge. 4. Collectively, to establish an ideal society in a propitious spot for the flowering of the new race, the race of the Sons of God."[12]

She has worked out this programme in intimate collaboration with Sri Aurobindo - once formulating their one divine personality as "mothersriaurobindo" in writing - and she has gone on working it out when alone in her avataric body. They had come to lay the foundations of the future and to build the archetype of the Supramental species. This is a rather well documented real story more fascinating than any myth, in which one sees the constant interaction of the three personalities of the Mother. In her conversations during the last years, as well as in the transformation of the cells of her physical body, it was unfortunately the human aspect that was most visible to human eyes.

Day by day and year after year Sri Aurobindo fought his occult and spiritual battles without anybody around him being aware of it; one only gets some glimpses of his "real work" in his poems and in *Savitri*. The Mother *has* spoken about her battles in the subconscient, her physical sufferings and some of her victories. But who was aware that that being sitting there in a simple armchair, on the first floor of the central Ashram building in Pondicherry, was no longer what the eyes perceived? Her back was bent and her visible body reduced to its elementary humanity; her invisible body within the visible one was glorious. On 24th March 1972 she said: "For the first time, early in the morning, I saw myself my body. I don't know whether it is a Supramental body or - how to say this? - a body in transition. But I had a body altogether new, in the sense that it was sexless, it wasn't a woman nor was it a man.[13] It was very white, but this is because my skin is white, I suppose,

____

12 The Mother: *Words of Long Ago, p.47.*

13 The Supramental body is a-sexual. Cf. talk 1: "Adam Kadmon and the Evolution".

I don't know. It was very slim ... It was pretty truly a harmonious form. So, this was the first time. I didn't know anything at all, I had no idea of what it would be like or whatever. And I saw that I *was* like that, I had *become* like that."

The tears and the desperation at the time of the Mother's passing were the human reaction resulting from the human perception of a life which had attempted and succeeded to incorporate, for the first time in the history of the Earth, the Supermind into Matter. She and Sri Aurobindo accomplished the impossible, so much beyond the human comprehension that their accomplishment today is a living reality to not more than a handful of followers. Her body - specially chosen and composed with care in her mother's womb, and declared by Sri Aurobindo to be better than his for the initial attempt at the Supramental transformation - her body lying there was not a cause for grief but the token of a triumph without precedent.

Coda

In *Champaklal Speaks* we read the following anecdote from the time the Mother still gave *darshan* on the balcony of the central Ashram building in the morning: "When Mother had her breakfast after 'Balcony', she said that she had come to know a very interesting thing. She had seen on the forehead of Mritunjoy's sister (who had just passed away), the symbol of Sri Aurobindo. Mother said that she was very much surprised and had said to herself: 'What? On this one?...' Then she heard Sri Aurobindo saying: 'Henceforth whoever who dies here (i.e. in the Ashram), I will put my seal upon him, and in any condition unconditional protection will be given."

We find this confirmed by the Mother herself in the *Agenda* conversation of 24th June 1961. Mritunjoy's sister was psychologically in a terrible state, said the Mother: *Elle n'avait pas la foi* - she did not have the faith. This led the Mother to ask Sri Aurobindo what happens to people who do not have the faith when they are in the Ashram and die there. Sri Aurobindo said: "Watch". The woman in question was in the act of leaving her body at that very moment, and the Mother "saw on her forehead the symbol of Sri Aurobindo in a kind of solid golden light ... And because of the presence of that symbol the psychological condition did not have any importance any more, for nothing could touch her." As we have seen, it is the psychological condition at the time of death which attracts the corresponding worlds and their beings. Then Sri Aurobindo said to the Mother: "All those who have lived in the Ashram and who die there have automatically the same protection, whatever their inner state."

At the time Auroville did not yet exist. Would it be unreasonable to surmise that a similar recognition and protection might be given to those who had the faith and surrendered their lives to the same ideal in Auroville?

Preparing for the Miraculous, eleven talks at Auroville,
Georges Van Vrekhem, 147-170

Sri Aurobindo's Descent into Death[1]

"The time is very serious"

In June 1946, less than a year after the unconditional surrender of Japan, Sri Aurobindo wrote: "There was a time when Hitler was victorious everywhere and it seemed certain that a black yoke of the Asura would be imposed on the whole world; but where is Hitler now and where is his rule? Berlin and Nuremberg (where in those days German top Nazis stood trial) have marked the end of that dreadful chapter in human history. Other blacknesses threaten to overshadow or even engulf mankind, but they too will end as that nightmare has ended." If one has the faintest notion of Sri Aurobindo and the Mother's decisive interventions in the Second World War, the fiercest and most deadly of all wars, and of its significance in human history, one has to be moved by these words. (The phrase "where is Hitler now?" may well be the softest worded victory bulletin ever.) But then, now that the war was won, why the sombre talk about other engulfing blacknesses which nobody else seemed to see? Yet the threat apparently increased, for in April of the following year Sri Aurobindo wrote: "Things are bad, are growing worse and may at any time grow worst or worse than worst if that is possible."

At that point, when Sri Aurobindo was seventy-five years old and after a lifetime of revolutionary avataric Yoga, something at the root of things was blocking the Work. Sri Aurobindo stated forcefully: "1 have no intention of giving my sanction to a new edition of the old fiasco - a partial and transient spiritual opening within with no true and radical change in the external nature." The old fiasco was the effort of the previous Avatars to change human nature and make spiritual progress in the material evolution possible. In his *Essays on the Gita* Sri Aurobindo had already written: "Not

---

1 This talk was given in Savitri Bhavan on 4 December 2010, in commemoration of the 60th anniversary of Sri Aurobindo's passing.

till the Time-Spirit in man is ready can the inner and ultimate prevail over the outer and immediate reality. Christ and Buddha have come and gone. But it is Rudra who still holds the world in the hollow of his hand. And meanwhile the fierce forward labour of mankind, tormented and oppressed by the Powers that are profiteers of egoistic force and their servants, cries for the sword of the Hero of the struggle and the word of the prophet."

It is said that Sri Aurobindo never explicitly stated that he was an Avatar. To expect such a statement would demand that Sri Aurobindo broke with his inborn and spiritual discretion. The quotations in the previous paragraph, however, make it abundantly clear, as do many other passages in his writings and acts in his workings, that he considered his yogic effort to be that of an Avatar, and even the most decisive of all avataric missions. On the other hand, where does one ever find a sign of the slightest awareness that in 1947 the Work of Sri Aurobindo and the Mother, on which the future of humanity depended, was threatened with annulment?

Nirodbaran, in those days with Champaklal the closest assistant of Sri Aurobindo and the Mother, wrote in his priceless *Twelve Years with Sri Aurobindo*: "We observed a noticeable change in his mood. Our talks ... diminished. He was no longer expansive; humour, wit, sally, fun, all had shrivelled up and we were in front of a temple deity, impassive, aloof and indifferent. However much we tried to draw him out from his impregnable sanctum of silence, we were answered with a monosyllabic 'yes' or 'no', or at most a faint smile.... One day taking courage in both hands, Dr.Satyendra asked: 'Why are you so serious, Sir?' Sri Aurobindo answered gravely: 'The time is very serious.' The answer left us mystified."

The decision

Things must have grown "worse than worst", for a drastic act became imperative. Of Sri Aurobindo's decision to perform this act nobody knew at the time. It is only afterwards that some sayings and facts could be seen as indicative of what was to happen. So for instance the following words of the Mother spoken to Dr.Sanyal on the very morning of Sri Aurobindo's passing: "About a year ago, while I was discussing things, I remarked that I felt like leaving this body of mine. Sri Aurobindo spoke out in a very firm tone: 'No, this can never be. If necessary for this transformation, I might go. You will have to fulfil our Yoga of Supramental descent and transformation.' ... After that - this took place early in 1950 - he gradually let himself fall ill for he knew quite well that, should he say 'I must go', I would not have obeyed him and I would have gone. For according to the way I felt, he was much more indispensable than I. But he saw the matter from the other side. And he knew that I had the power to leave my body at will. So he didn't say a thing - he didn't say a thing right to the very last minute."

Later the Mother would concede: "It is absolutely undeniable that my body has that capacity (of endurance) infinitely more than the body of Sri Aurobindo." This reminds us of her former saying that she had consciously chosen her parents not only for their mental but also for their physical qualities. She also said later: "I told him that, as to me, it would be absolutely without regret and without difficulty that I would leave my body to go and join him ... And he answered: 'Your body is indispensable for the Work. Without your body the Work cannot be done.' This is something that was said in 1949, which means a little more than a year before he left."

Then there is the amazing avowal of the Mother that she does not seem to have known that Sri Aurobindo, step by invisible step, let death approach. She has confirmed this more than once herself. For instance: "You see, he had decided to go. But he didn't want me to know that he was doing it deliberately. He knew that if for a single moment I knew he was doing it deliberately, I would have reacted with such violence that he would not have been able to leave. And he did this: he bore it all as if it was some unconsciousness, an ordinary illness, simply to keep me from knowing - and he left at the very moment he had to leave." Sri Aurobindo had created a blind spot, as it were, in the perception of her who was the Mother of the worlds and had access to all knowledge everywhere if she so desired! Once she said: "I did not believe till the last moment that Sri Aurobindo was going to leave his body." And K.D.Sethna commented: "This is correct. On December 3rd (Sri Aurobindo passed away on the 5th) the Mother told me that Sri Aurobindo would soon read my articles. Later, when I asked her why she had let me go to Bombay on December 3rd, she said that Sri Aurobindo's going had not been decided yet."

Initially, except for some minor symptoms of kidney trouble, there were no signs of serious health problems whatever. Besides, Sri Aurobindo continued his (outwardly) daily routine as if nothing was the matter. He still wanted to write on modem poetry and a search was on to provide him with volumes of such poetry to read. (He appreciated Mallarme, Whitman, Yeats and Eliot.) He also dictated, at the Mother's request, the important series of articles published under the title *The Supramental Manifestation upon Earth*.

In these articles he expounded the state of affairs at that time of his Work, of his Yoga of Transformation, explaining the realization of the "Mind of Light", and the necessity of a range of intermediary beings between the present human and the future Supramental species. These transitional specics or subspecies in the making he gave no name, calling them in general "a new humanity". The Mother, however, did give them a name in French, *"surhommes"*, literally meaning "overmen". She said: "This was certainly what he expected of us: what he conceived of as the overman, who must be the intermediate being between humanity as it is and the Supramental being created in the Supramental way ... It is quite obvious that intermediary beings are necessary, and that it is these intermediary beings who must find the means to create beings of the Supermind. And there is no doubt that, when Sri Aurobindo wrote this, he was convinced that this is what we have to do."

Somewhere in October, solicited from many sides, Sri Aurobindo said to Nirodbaran: "My main work is being delayed." For, as Nirodbaran wrote: "Many interruptions came in the way. The preliminary work of reading old versions, selections, etc (of Sri Aurobindo's own writings being prepared for publication), took up much time before we actually could start i.e. continue working on *Savitri*." Still the urgency in Sri Aurobindo's remark startled Nirodbaran, as he had never seen Sri Aurobindo hurry for anything. "When the last revision was made and the Cantos were wound up, I said: 'It is finished now.' An impersonal smile of satisfaction greeted me, and he said: 'Ah, is it finished?' How well I remember that flicker of a smile which all of us craved for so long! 'What is left now?' was his next query. 'The Book of Death and the Epilogue'. 'Oh, that? We shall see about that later on.' That 'later on' never came and was not meant to come." For the subject matter of *Savitri* were the experiences of Sri Aurobindo and the Mother. Death had not yet been experienced. And the Epilogue, the happy ending which in this case will be a life of fulfilment on Earth, lies somewhere in the future. Thus reached Savitri, in the words of Nirodbaran, its "incomplete completion".

The "worse than worst" situation did not subside. The ureamic symptoms increased, for the moment of the great master act of the Avatar had come. After all the work Sri Aurobindo and the Mother had done, after all the burdens and the suffering, the black passages and the dawns of light, something had to be done which is unknown of in the history of humankind. As the Mother would say later: "For the Will of the Supreme to be expressed as it were in contradiction with the totality of the laws of the Manifestation, that happens just at the last moment - at the ultimate limit of possibility."

The descent into death

Sri Aurobindo's "death" was interpreted by most as the natural result of illness and/or advanced age.

In 1924 Sri Aurobindo had said that there were three causes that (then) could still bring about his death: 1. violent surprise or accident; 2. the action of old age; 3. his own choice, when finding it not possible to accomplish his (avataric) endeavour this time i.e. establishing the Supramental Consciousness on Earth, or if something would prove to him that it was impossible. What happened in 1950, however, was a fourth possibility not foreseeable in 1924: that he would have to descend into death voluntarily, having in the meantime acquired the powers to do so, in order to make sure that his endeavour would not end in failure.

Who realized in December 1950 - and even now - that at that time, in that place on Earth, a mystery without precedence was enacted on which humanity's future depended?

This "tactical" move was possible because the Avatar was present on Earth in his/her physical completeness i.e. in a male/female body. If the Avatar had been present in only one body, the death of this body would have cancelled out any possibility of accomplishing the present mission successfully. (This illustrates how the planning and the completion of the mission of an Avatar is decided upon and pre-exists outside the dimensions, outside "the theatre" of the material world.)

Sri Aurobindo let himself gradually become more and more ill. In the last few days before his departure the Mother said: "He is losing interest in himself." The faithful Nirodbaran, gathering his courage in both hands, ventured at last to ask him: "Are you not using your force to cure yourself?" "No!" came the stunning reply.... Then, Nirodbaran writes, we asked: "Why not? How is the disease going to be cured otherwise?" "Can't explain. You won't understand," was the curt reply. On this Nirodbaran reflects: "The big mystery as to his strange attitude and non-intervention still remains." None understood, then as now, that Sri Aurobindo descended voluntarily into death to do something in the Inconscient which only the Avatar could execute, in order to prevent that his mission on Earth, in the short or the long term, would come to nothing.

According to the testimony of Nirodbaran, a medical doctor, Sri Aurobindo was never unconscious in the course of his "illness". "It was during this period (on the very last day) that he often came out of the trance and each time leaned forward, hugged and kissed Champaklal who was sitting by the side of his bed. Champaklal also hugged him in return. A wonderful sight it was, though so strangely unlike Sri Aurobindo who had rarely called us even by our names in these twelve years." The Avatar took leave of humanity in one of its purest representatives.

At 11 p.m. on the 4th of December the Mother helped Sri Aurobindo take a drink. At midnight she carne again into his room. This time he opened his eyes and the two looked at each other in a steady gaze. "We were the silent spectators of that crucial scene," writes Nirodbaran.

At 1 a.m. on the 5th of December the Mother came again. Her face was calm, there was no trace of emotion. Sri Aurobindo was indrawn. The Mother asked Dr.Sanyal in a quiet tone: "What do you think? May I retire for an hour? ... Call me when the time comes." On this Nirodbaran reflects: "It may appear strange to our human mind that the Mother could leave Sri Aurobindo at this critical moment." Yet, the Mother's clarification is quite different: "As long as I was in the room he could not leave his body. I used all my power to prevent him from departing. So there was a terrible tension in him: the inner will to leave and then this kind of thing i.e. the Mother, that was holding him there, like that, in his body - because I knew that he was alive ... He had to give a sign so that I would go into my room, supposedly to rest (which I didn't do). And as soon as I had gone out of the room, he left." He drew up his arms and put them on his chest, one overlapping the other. "Then they called me back immediately."

Soon afterwards the main personalities in the Ashram were informed and the Ashram photographers called before the endless queue would form to pay their last homage. Two of the photographers' testimonies are worth comparing.

The first one recalls: "I remember clearly that Mother was sitting in the middle room beside Sri Aurobindo's, where the tiger skins and the Mother's paintings are displayed. She looked very dejected. She was stooping with a hand on her forehead, and did not notice me as I entered."

The second photographer, on the contrary, recalls: "When I entered Sri Aurobindo's abode through the door at the top of the staircase leading from the Meditation Hall, I instantly became petrified by the sight of the Mother sitting on a chair in the central room - the room in which her paintings adorn the walls and the tiger skins decorate the divan. She was seated between the two doors on the southern side of the narrow room with her eyes shut, lost in deep meditation. I have never seen her like that again. To me she looked like the personification of Mother Kali herself, so powerful was the appearance. I stood before her for some time."

The Mind of Light

On the last day before Sri Aurobindo left his body the Mother said: "Each time I enter the room, I see him pulling down the Supramental Light." And later: "All the Supramental force he had accumulated in his body, he passed on to me and I received it."

In his memoir *A Call from Pondicherry*, Dr.Prabhat Sanyal wrote: "She stood there, near the feet of Sri Aurobindo, her hair had been undressed and was flowing about her shoulders." Once again, to know what really happened in those climactic hours, we have to turn to the Mother herself. "He had accumulated in his body much Supramental Force, and as soon as he left ... You see, he was lying on his bed, I stood by his side, and in a way altogether concrete - concrete with such a strong sensation as to make one think that it could be seen - all this Supramental Force which was in him passed from his body into mine. And I felt the friction of the passage. It was extraordinary. It was an extraordinary experience.... When he left, there was a whole part - the most material part of the 'descent' (the formation in Sri Aurobindo) of the Supramental body up to the (physical) mental - which visibly came out of his body, like this (gesture), and entered into mine. And this was so concrete that I felt the friction of the forces passing through the pores of the skin. It was as concrete as if it had been material."

Here it should be recalled that Sri Aurobindo and the Mother had divided the tasks for the accomplishment of their mission. Sri Aurobindo, secluded in his apartment, took upon him the Yoga of bringing down the Supermind into his physical body. As his physical body, like any other human body, was a formation of the terrestrial evolution, this also meant that he was bringing down the Supermind in the very stuff of the Earth.

The Mother had taken upon her the building up of the Ashram, materially as well as spiritually, and the yoga of the *sadhaks* and *sadhikas* who, as she once said, were enclosed in her consciousness "as in an egg". Yet every new realization in his Yoga Sri Aurobindo transmitted to her, and everything that went on in the Ashram the Mother submitted to Sri Aurobindo. This "division of the tasks" is essential to understand what happened between them at the time of Sri Aurobindo's departure.

"As soon as Sri Aurobindo withdrew from his body, what he has called the Mind of Light got realized in me," the Mother said afterwards to K.D.Sethna. "The Supermind had descended long ago - very long ago - into the mind and even into the vital; it was working in the physical also but indirectly through those intermediaries. The question was about the direct action of the Supermind in the physical. Sri Aurobindo said it could be possible only if the physical mind received the Supramental light: the physical mind was the instrument for direct action upon the most material. The physical mind receiving the Supramental light Sri Aurobindo called the Mind of Light."

Sri Aurobindo's leaving the body meant a traumatic change for the Mother in ways we cannot even try to imagine. Which human can have an idea of the relationship between the embodied Ishwara and Shakti? "There are no words which can describe the collapse that has been for it," said the Mother later, and by "it" she meant her body. It had been *un coup de massue*, a sledgehammer blow ... "When Sri Aurobindo had left, I saw that I had to cut the connection with the psychic being, otherwise I would have gone with him. And as I had promised him that I would stay on and do the work, I had to do that: I literally closed the door on the psychic." It would take almost two decades before she could venture, in 1969, to open that door again.

What was threatening the accomplishment of the avataric mission?

In *The Life Divine* Sri Aurobindo wrote: "There can be no artificial escape from this problem (evil, suffering and death) which has always troubled humanity and from which it has found no satisfying issue. The tree of the knowledge of good and evil with its sweet and bitter fruits is secretly rooted in the very nature of the Inconscience from which our being has emerged and on which it still stands as a nether soil and basis of our physical existence ... There can be no final solution until we have turned our Inconscience into the greater consciousness, made the truth of self and spirit our life-basis and transformed our ignorance into a higher knowledge; a complete and radical transformation of our nature is the only true solution." Only Supermind would do. But the bringing down of the Supermind into the body of the Earth, the complete and radical transformation of our nature, was precisely what the hostile forces were trying to prevent at any cost, for it would mean the end of their dominion over the Earth and humanity.

One reads of many masters in several yogic disciplines who possessed the power to lay down their body at will. The difference with Sri Aurobindo's master act was that he went into death in full consciousness and while keeping the vital and mental sheaths which, let us not forget it, were Supramentally transformed. And this he did not in search of escape or dissolution, but to intervene and effect a change somewhere at the bottom of existence, in what he called "the Inconscient", worse than hell. "He was not compelled to leave his body," said the Mother. "He chose to do so for reasons so sublime that they are beyond the reach of human mentality."

But why? The Mother's "*Pourquoi?*" resounds in so many of her conversations. "He has left before telling us what he was doing. I am absolutely busy making a path in a virgin forest - more than a virgin forest." (Perhaps she was not allowed to know because she - her body - had to do the job. It may not have been permitted to have a knowledge beyond its effort.) "He told me: 'The world is not ready.'" It looks as if "the world" here means the whole of the manifestation at this point of its evolution. For that was the burden the Avatar had to take upon him, which needed to be transformed in its foundations, and which kept resisting him.

In his marvellous poem "*A God's Labour*" - which might also be called "The Avatar's Song" or "The Ballad of the Avatar" - Sri Aurobindo had described exactly this problem.

> *A voice cried, "Go where none has gone!*
> *   Dig deeper, deeper yet*
> *Till you reach the grim foundation stone*
> *   And knock at the keyless gate."*
> *I saw that falsehood was planted deep*
> *   At the very root of things*
> *Where the grey Sphinx guards God's riddle sleep*
> *   On the Dragon's outspread wings.*

True, "the keyless gate", "the grey Sphinx" and "the Dragon's outspread wings", all concrete elements of his experience, are little more than poetic metaphors to us. But "God's riddle sleep" is clearly the dark Inconscient, and that was what Sri Aurobindo descended into for an operation which only the Avatar, the very Divine, could perform. We find something similar in his sonnet "The Inconscient Foundation":

> *My soul regards its veiled subconscient base,*
> *   All the dead obstinate symbols of the past,*
> *The hereditary moulds, the stamps of race*
> *   Are upheld to sight, the old imprints effaced.*
> *In a downpour of supernal light it reads*
> *   The black Inconscient's enigmatic script recorded*
> *In a hundred shadowy screeds*

> *An inert world's obscure enormous drift.*
> *There slept the tables of the Ignorance,*
> *There the dumb dragon edicts of her sway,*
> *The scriptures of Necessity and Chance.*

In *Savitri* we find Sri Aurobindo again confronting "the black inertia of our base" and seeking for "the secret key of Nature's change:"

> *The ordeal he suffered of evil's absolute reign ...*
> *Incapable of motion or of force,*
> *In Matter's blank denial goaled and blind,*
> *Pinned to the black inertia of our base*
> *He treasured between his hands his flickering soul.*
> *Into the abysmal secrecy he came*
> *Where darkness peers from her mattress, grey and nude,*
> *And stood on the last locked subconscient's floor*
> *Where Being slept unconscious of its thoughts*
> *And built the world not knowing what it built.*
> *He saw the secret key of Nature's change.*

Then...

> *Torn were the formats of the primal Night*
> *And shattered the stereotypes of the Ignorance.*
> *He imposed upon dark atom and dumb mass*
> *The diamond script of the Imperishable*
> *Matter and Spirit mingled and were one.*

As the Mother said: "All goes well as long as there is not the will of transformation. It is the protest against the will of transformation. It is the introduction of something totally new into Matter, and therefore the body protests ... There is a whole part of Nature which is collaborating, but not in this. Distinctly, clearly, it wells up from the subconscient and the inconscient. ... It's something that wells up from below ... All the time it comes up from below." This was the reason why Sri Aurobindo had to descend into death. That he was successful, that he found the key to the impossible and cured the source of darkness at the bottom of things, we know from the fact that hardly six years later the Supermind manifested in the Earth atmosphere, and a new world was born.

Triumph

There is no known person who at the time of Sri Aurobindo's passing had the slightest inkling of what was happening. "You wouldn't understand," he had said. We have seen how, during that extraordinary episode, the behaviour of Sri Aurobindo and the Mother also was time and again misinterpreted in a too human way - misinterpretations which, written down by the eye-witnesses, would become part of the standard story built around the event. If we know a little better now, if we have at least some ground for a more meaningful interpretation, it is because the Mother in later years has reminisced about those days on several occasions.

The result of the lack of understanding was, in many, doubt and desperation. What use was it to continue dedicating one's life to a Supramental transformation and the conquest of death when the Guru, or Master, or Avatar and bringer of the new vision had succumbed himself to death? Therefore the Mother gave the following message on the 14th of December: "To grieve is an insult to Sri Aurobindo, who is here with us, conscious and alive."

At least there had been signs that Sri Aurobindo had not left in the ordinary way. Nirodbaran wrote in his Twelve Years: "I also saw, to my utter wonder and delight, that the entire body was suffused with a golden crimson hue, so fresh, so magnificent. It seemed to have lifted my pall of gloom and I felt light and happy without knowing why.... Pointing to the Light the Mother said: 'If this Supramental Light remains we shall keep the body in a glass case.' It did not remain, and on the fifth day, on the 9th of December in the evening, the body was laid in a vault."

And K.D.Sethna, many years afterwards, would write in Mother India, the Ashram periodical of which he was the editor: "I marked that there was nothing like what people usually speak of when they stand before someone dead. They refer to the expression of peace on the face. I saw the very opposite. Certainly not any stamp of agitation but the unmoving source of a sovereign dynamism. A tremendous power seemed to emanate from the face and figure. Wave after wave of it filled the room and surrounded me. I perceived an overwhelming air of Conquest ... From the flaring nostrils to the way in which the legs were stretched out, slightly apart, there was a natural aspect of domination. Spontaneously, effortlessly an assertion of empire could be experienced. Here was a silence, transcendent of all creation - an ultimate absolute of the ineffable - from which originally had flowed forth a creative energy and which now was sending out a power of re-creating all life. Such was the mysterious death of Sri Aurobindo." The poet that was K.D.Sethna had seen better than most of his less intuitive co-disciples.

"What we are doing will be a beginning, not a completion," Sri Aurobindo had written in a letter. He, as no one else, knew how difficult his envisioned transformation of *Homo sapiens* actually was, beginning with the bringing down of the Supermind into the body of the Earth and continuing with the transformation of the human body, as it were petrified in its evolutionary structures. The manifestation of the Supermind had been felt to be imminent in 1938-39, a possibility which may be reckoned as the main reason of the fierce counteraction by the hostile forces: the Second World War. At that point Sri Aurobindo was not even confronted by the possibility of the "fiasco" which threatened his and the Mother's mission. This may give us at least some idea of the dimensions of the whole enterprise and of the greatness of the two Protagonists who stood up, Sri Aurobindo in 1950 and the Mother in the following years, against the assembled Powers still holding the entire manifestation in the palm of their hand.

Now we are further again. Sri Aurobindo's intervention at the root of things has enabled the manifestation of the Supermind in 1956. His words about the capability of the Mother's body have proved true, and in the following years she has gradually realized the archetype of the Supramental body by means of her physical body. By these two realizations the appearance of the next step in the evolution, the Supramental being, has been brought nearer by centuries if not millennia. Ours, humans of goodwill and aspiration, is the task of the intermediaries between the two species, of building the bridge over an enormous evolutionary gap.

In this we are not alone. If we can tune ourselves to them, we are helped by four powerful aids: the Supramental Force, active since 1956; the Consciousness of the Overman, active since 1st January 1969; Sri Aurobindo's presence; and the Mother's presence. For Sri Aurobindo's and the Mother's work of building the New World cannot have been limited to their years of incarnation in a physical body. Helpers of the progress of the Earth and humanity during the whole of the past, they are undoubtedly there to help them now, after their initiation of the new evolution in its critical present phase.

Preparing for the Miraculous, eleven talks at Auroville,
Georges Van Vrekhem, 171-189

Sri Aurobindo on Rebirth

The soul takes birth each time, and each time a mind, life and body are formed out of the materials of universal nature according to the soul's past evolution and its need for the future.

When the body is dissolved, the vital goes into the vital plane and remains there for a time, but after a time the vital sheath disappears. The last to dissolve is the mental sheath. Finally the soul or psychic being retires into the psychic world to rest there till a new birth is close.

This is the general course for ordinarily developed human beings. There are variations according to the nature of the individual and his development. For example, if the mental is strongly developed, then the mental being can remain; so also can the vital, provided they are organized by and centred around the true psychic being; they share the immortality of the psychic.

The soul gathers the essential elements of its experiences in life and makes that its basis of growth in the evolution; when it returns to birth it takes up with its mental, vital, physical sheaths so much of its Karma as is useful to it in the new life for further experience.

It is really for the vital part of the being that *śrāddha* and rites are done - to help the being to get rid of the vital vibrations which still attach it to the earth or to the vital worlds, so that it may pass quickly to its rest in the psychic peace.

I only said what was originally meant by the ceremonies - the rites. I was not referring to the feeding of the caste or the Brahmins which is not a rite or ceremony. Whether *śrāddha* as performed is actually effective is another matter - for those who perform it have not either the knowledge or the occult power.

After leaving the body, the soul, after certain experiences in other worlds, throws off its mental and vital personalities and goes into rest to assimilate the essence of its past and prepare for a new life. It is this preparation that determines the circumstances of the new birth and guides it in its reconstitution of a new personality and the choice of its materials.

The departed soul retains the memory of its past experiences only in their essence, not in their form or detail. It is only if the soul brings back some past personality or personalities as part of its present manifestation that it is likely to remember the details of the past life. Otherwise, it is only by Yogadrishti that the memory comes.

The Karana-purusha is what is called the central being by us, the Jiva. It stands above the play, supporting it always.

There may be what seems to be retrograde movements but these are only like zigzag movements, not a real falling back, but a return on something not worked out so as to go on better afterwards. The soul does not go back to the animal condition; but a part of the vital personality may disjoin itself and join an animal birth to work out its animal propensities there.

There is no truth in the popular belief about the avaricious man becoming a serpent. These are popular romantic superstitions.

The soul after it leaves the body travels through several states or planes until the psychic being has shed its temporary sheaths, then it reaches the psychic world where it rests in a kind of sleep till it is ready for reincarnation. What it keeps with it of the human experience in the end is only the essence of all that it has gone through, what it can use for its development. This is the general rule, but it does not apply to exceptional cases or to very developed beings who have achieved a greater consciousness than the ordinary human level.

It is not the soul (the psychic being) that takes a lesser form, it is some part of the manifested being, usually some part of the vital that does it, owing to some desire, affinity, need of particular experience. This happens fairly often to the ordinary man.

—

The soul goes out, after death, in a subtle body. Recollections last only for a time, not till rebirth - otherwise the stamp would be so strong that remembrance of past births, even after taking a new body, would be the rule rather than the exception.

You say "relationships of one birth persist in successive births, the chances depending on the strength of the attachment." This is possible, but not a law - as a rule the same relationship would not be constantly repeated - the same people often meet again and again on earth in different lives, but the relations are different. The purpose of rebirth would not be served if the same personality with the same relations and experiences are incessantly repeated.

It is not the case that there is complete annihilation of the ego in respect of forms of life lower than man after death. What was spoken of as being in a static condition of complete rest is not the ego, but the psychic being after it has shed its vital and other sheaths and is resting in the psychic world. Before that it passes through vital and other worlds on its way to the psychic plane.

It is possible to come into direct touch with the departed so long as they are near enough to the earth (it is usually supposed by those who have occult experience that it is for three years only) or if they are earthbound or if they are of those who do not proceed to the psychic plane but linger near the earth and are soon reborn.

Universal statements cannot be easily made about these things - there is a general line, but individual cases vary to an almost indefinite extent.

—

There is after death a period in which one passes through the vital world and lives there for a time. It is only the first part of this transit that can be dangerous or painful; in the rest one works out, under certain surroundings, the remnant of the vital desires and instincts which one had in the body. As soon as one is tired of these and able to go beyond, the vital sheath is dropped and the soul after a time needed to get rid of some mental survivals passes into a state of rest in the psychic world and remains there till the next life on earth.

One can help the departed souls by one's good will or by occult means, if one has the knowledge. The one thing that one should not do is to hold them back by sorrow for them or longings or by anything else that would pull them nearer to earth or delay their journey to their place of rest.

—

It may happen to some not to realise for a little time that they are dead, especially if the death has been unforeseen and sudden, but it cannot be said that it happens to all or to most. Some may enter into a state of semi-unconsciousness or obsession by a dark inner condition created by their state of mind at death, in which they realise nothing of where they are, etc; others are quite conscious of the passage. It is true that the departing being in the vital body lingers for some time near the body or the scene of life very often for as many as eight days and, in the ancient religions, mantras and other means were used for the severance. Even after the severance from the body a very earthbound nature or one full of strong physical desires may linger long in the earth-atmosphere up to a maximum period extended to three years.

Afterwards, it passes to the vital worlds, proceeding on its journey which must sooner or later bring it to the psychic rest till the next life. It is true also that sorrow and mourning for the dead impede their progress by keeping them tied to the earth-atmosphere and pulling them back from their passage.

—

It is necessary to understand clearly the difference between the evolving soul (psychic being) and the pure Atman, self or spirit. The pure self is unborn, does not pass through death or birth, is independent of birth or body, mind or life or this manifested Nature. It is not bound by these things, not limited, not affected, even though it assumes and supports them. The soul, on the contrary, is something that comes down into birth and passes through death - although it does not itself die, for it is immortal - from one state to another, from the earth plane to other planes and back again to the earth-existence. It goes on with this progression from life to life through an evolution which leads it up to the human state and evolves through it all a being of itself which we call the psychic being that supports the evolution and develops a physical, a vital, a mental human consciousness as its instruments of world-experience and of a disguised, imperfect, but growing self-expression. All this it does from behind a veil showing something of its divine self only in so far as the imperfection of the instrumental being will allow it. But a time comes when it is able to prepare to come out from behind the veil, to take command and turn all the instrumental nature towards a divine fulfilment. This is the beginning of the true spiritual life. The soul is able now to make itself ready for a higher evolution of manifested consciousness than the mental human - it can pass from the mental to the spiritual and through degrees of the spiritual to the Supramental state. Till then there is no reason why it should cease from birth, it cannot in fact do so. If having reached the spiritual state, it wills to pass out of the terrestrial manifestation, it may indeed do so - but there is also possible a higher manifestation, in the Knowledge and not in the Ignorance.

Your question therefore does not arise. It is not the naked spirit, but the psychic being that goes to the psychic plane to rest till it is called again to another life. There is, therefore, no need of a Force to compel it to take birth anew. It is in its nature something that is put forth from the Divine to support the evolution and it must do so till the Divine's purpose in its evolution is accomplished. Karma is only a machinery, it is not the fundamental cause of terrestrial existence - it cannot be, for when the soul first entered this existence, it had no Karma.

What again do you mean by "the all-veiling Maya" or by "losing all consciousness"? The soul cannot lose all consciousness, for its very nature is consciousness though not of the mental kind to which we give the name. The consciousness is merely covered, not lost or abolished by the so-called Inconscience of material Nature and then by the half-conscious ignorance of mind, life and body. It manifests, as the individual mind and life and body grow, as much as may be of the consciousness which it holds in potentiality, manifests it in the outward instrumental nature as far as and in the way that is possible through these instruments and through the outer personality that has been prepared for it and by it - for both are true - for the present life.

I know nothing about any terrible suffering endured by the soul in the process of rebirth; popular beliefs even when they have some foundation are seldom enlightened and accurate.

1. The psychic being stands behind mind, life and body, supporting them; so also the psychic world is not one world in the scale like the mental, vital or physical worlds, but stands behind all these and it is there that the souls evolving here retire for the time between life and life. If the psychic were only one principle in the rising order of body, life and mind on a par with the others and placed somewhere in the scale on the same footing as the others, it could not be the soul of all the rest, the divine element making the evolution of the others possible and using them as instruments for a growth through cosmic experience towards the Divine. So also the psychic world cannot be one among the other worlds to which the evolutionary being goes for supraphysical experience; it is a plane where it retires into itself for rest, for a spiritual assimilation of what it has experienced and for a replunging

into its own fundamental consciousness and psychic nature.

2. For the few who go out of the Ignorance and enter into Nirvana, there is no question of their going straight up into higher worlds of manifestation. Nirvana or Moksha is a liberated condition of the being, not a world - it is a withdrawal from the worlds and the manifestation. The analogy of *pitryiina* and *devayiina* can hardly be mentioned in this connection.

3. The condition of the souls that retire into the psychic world is entirely static; each withdraws into himself and is not interacting with the others. When they come out of their trance, they are ready to go down into a new life, but meanwhile they do not act upon the earth life. There are other beings, guardians of the psychic world, but they are concerned only with the psychic world itself and the return of the souls to reincarnation, not with the earth.

4. A being of a psychic world cannot get fused into the soul of a human being on earth. What happens in some cases is that a very advanced psychic being sometimes sends down an emanation which resides in a human being and prepares it until it is ready for the psychic being itself to enter into the life. This happens when some special work has to be done and the human vehicle prepared. Such a descent produces a remarkable change of a sudden character in the personality and the nature.

5. Usually, a soul follows continuously the same line of sex. If there are shiftings of sex, it is, as a rule, a matter of parts of the personality which are not central.

6. As regards the stage at which the soul returning for re-birth enters the new body no rule can be laid down, for the circumstances vary with the individual. Some psychic beings get into relation with the birth-environment and the parents from the time of conception and determine the preparation of the personality and future in the embryo, others join only at the time of delivery, others even later on in the life and in these cases it is some emanation of the psychic being which upholds the life. It should be noted that the conditions of the future birth are determined fundamentally not during the stay in the

psychic world but at the time of death - the psychic being then chooses what it should work out in the next terrestrial appearance and the conditions arrange themselves accordingly.

Note that the idea of rebirth and the circumstances of the new life as a reward or punishment of *punya* or *papa* is a crude human idea of "justice" which is quite unphilosophical and unspiritual and distorts the true intention of life. Life here is an evolution and the soul grows by experience, working out by it this or that in the nature, and if there is suffering, it is for the purpose of that working out, not as a judgment inflicted by God or Cosmic Law on the errors or stumblings which are inevitable in the Ignorance.

Sri Aurobindo, Letters on Yoga, Vol. I, pp.433-441

Sri Aurobindo's Protection after death

Henceforth whoever dies here, I will put my seal upon him and in any condition, unconditional protection will be given.

Felicity Eternal, p.90: CH Speaks: 135

Death is not a way to succeed in sadhana. If you die in that way, you will only have the same difficulties again with probably less favourable circumstances.

The way to succeed in sadhana is to refuse to be discouraged, to aspire simply and sincerely so that the Mother's force may work in you and bring down what is above. No man ever succeeded in this sadhana by his own merit. To become open and plastic to the Mother is the one thing needed.

That is not right. Throwing away the life does not improve the chances for the next time. It is in this life and body that one must get things done.

Sri Aurobindo, Letters On Yoga, Vol. III, p.747

The 1919 Flu in Japan

I was in Japan. It was at the beginning of January 1919. Anyway, it was the time when a terrible flu raged there in the whole of Japan, which killed hundreds of thousands of people. It was one of those epidemics the like of which is rarely seen. In Tokyo, every day there were hundreds and hundreds of new cases. The disease appeared to take this turn: it lasted three days and on the third day the patient died. And people died in such large numbers that they could not even be cremated, you understand, it was impossible, there were too many of them. Or otherwise, if one did not die on the third day, at the end of seven days one was altogether cured; a little exhausted but all the same completely cured. There was a panic in the town, for epidemics are very rare in Japan. They are a very clean people, very careful and with a fine morale. Illnesses are very rare. But still this came, it came as a catastrophe. There was a terrible fear. For example, people were seen walking about in the streets with a mask on the nose, a mask to purify the air they were breathing, so that it might not be full of the microbes of the illness. It was a common fear... Now, it so happened I was living with someone who never ceased troubling me: "But what is this disease? What is there behind this disease?" What I was doing, you know, was simply to cover myself with my force, my protection so as not to catch it and I did not think of it any more and continued doing my work. Nothing happened and I was not thinking of it. But constantly I heard: "What is this? Oh. I would like to know what is there behind this illness. But could you not tell me what this illness is, why it is there?..." etc. One day I was called to the other end of the town by a young woman whom I knew and who wished to introduce me to some friends and show me certain things: I do not remember now what exactly was the matter, but anyway I had to cross the whole town in a tram-car. And I was in the tram and seeing these people with masks on their noses, and then there was in the atmosphere this constant fear, and so there came a suggestion to me; I began to ask myself: "Truly, what

1917, Kyoto, Japan

is this illness? What is there behind this illness? What are the forces that are in this illness?…" I came to the house, I passed an hour there and I returned. And I returned with a terrible fever. I had caught it. It came to you thus, without preparation, instantaneously. Illnesses, generally illnesses from germs and microbes, take a few days in the system: they come, there is a little battle inside; you win or you lose, if you lose you catch the illness, it is not complicated. But there, you just receive a letter, open the envelope, hop! puff! The next minute you have the fever. Well, that evening I had a terrible fever. The doctor was called (it was not I who called him), the doctor was called and he told me: "I must absolutely give you this medicine." It was one of the best medicines for the fever, he had just a little (all their stocks were exhausted, everyone was taking it); he said: "I have still a few packets, I shall give you some" … "I beg of you, do not give it to me, I won't take it. Keep it for someone who has faith in it and will take it." He was quite disgusted: "It was no use my coming here." So I said: "Perhaps it was no use!" And I remained in my bed, with my fever, a violent fever. All the while I was asking myself: "What is this illness? Why is it there? What is there behind it?…" At the end of the second day, as I was lying all alone, I saw clearly a being, with a part of the head cut off, in a military uniform (or the remains of a military uniform) approaching me and suddenly flinging himself upon my chest, with that half a head to suck my force. I took a good look, then realised that I was about to die. He was drawing all my life out (for I must tell you that people were dying of pneumonia in three days). I was completely nailed to the bed, without movement, in a deep trance. I could no longer stir and he was pulling. I thought: now it is the end. Then I called on my occult power, I gave a big fight and I succeeded in turning him back so that he could not stay there any longer. And I woke up.

But I had seen. And I had learnt, I had understood that the illness originated from beings who had been thrown out of their bodies. I had seen this during the First Great War, towards its end, when people used to live in trenches and were killed by bombardment. They were in perfect health, altogether healthy, and in a second they were thrown out of their bodies, not conscious that they were dead. They did not know they hadn't a body any more and they tried to find in others the life they could not find in themselves. That is, they were turned into so many countless vampires. And they vampirised upon men. And then over and above that, there was a decomposition of the vital forces of people who fell ill and died. One lived in a kind of sticky and thick cloud made up of all that. And so those who took in this cloud fell ill and usually got cured, but those who were attacked by a being of that kind invariably died, they could not resist. I know how much knowledge and force were necessary for me to resist. It was irresistible. That is, if they were attacked by a being who was a centre of this whirl of bad forces, they died. And there must have been many of these, a very great number. I saw all that and I understood.

When someone came to see me, I asked to be left alone, I lay quietly in my bed and I passed two or three days absolutely quiet, in concentration, with my consciousness. Subsequently, a friend of ours (a Japanese, a very good friend) came and told me: "Ah! you were ill? So what I thought was true... Just imagine for the last two or three days, there hasn't been a single new case of illness in the town and most of the people who were ill have been cured and the number of deaths has become almost negligible, and now it is all over. The illness is wholly under control." Then I narrated what had happened to me and he went and narrated it to everybody. They even published articles about it in the papers.

Well, consciousness, to be sure, is more effective than packets of medicine!... The condition was critical. Just imagine, there were entire villages where everyone had died. There was a village in Japan, not very big, but still with more than a hundred people, and it happened, due to an extraordinary chance, that one of the villagers was to receive a letter (the postman went there only if there was a letter; naturally, it was a village far in the countryside); so he went to the countryside; there was a snowfall; the whole village was under snow... and there was not a living person. It was exactly so. It was that kind of epidemic. And Tokyo was also like that; but Tokyo was a big town and things did not happen in the same fashion. And it was in this way the epidemic ended. That is my story.

The 1918 flu pandemic (commonly referred to as the Spanish Flu) was an influenza pandemic that spread to nearly every part of the world. It was caused by an unusually virulent and deadly influenza, a virus strain of subtype H1N1. Historical and epidemiological data are inadequate to identify the geographic origin of the virus. Most of its victims were healthy young adults, in contrast to most influenza outbreaks which predominantly affect juvenile, elderly, or otherwise weakened patients. The flu pandemic has also been implicated in the sudden outbreak of encephalitis lethargica in the 1920s.

The pandemic lasted from March 1918 to June 1920, spreading even to the Arctic and remote Pacific islands. It is estimated that anywhere from 50 to 100 million people were killed worldwide, which is from three to seven times the casualties of the First World War (15 million), making it the most deadly natural disaster in human history. An estimated 50 million people, about 3% of the world's population (approximately 1.6 billion at the time), died of the disease. An estimated 500 million, or 1/3 were infected.

The global mortality rate from the 1918/1919 pandemic is not known, but it is estimated that 10% to 20% of those who were infected died. With about a third of the world population infected, this case fatality ratio means that 3% to 6% of the entire global population died. Influenza may have killed as many as 25 million in its first 25 weeks. Older estimates say it killed 40–50 million people, while current estimates say 50-100 million people worldwide were killed. This pandemic has been described as "the greatest medical holocaust in history" and may have killed more people than the Black Death.

As many as 17 million died in India, about 5% of India's population at the time. In Japan, 23 million people were affected, and 390,000 died. Wikipedia, Encyclopedia

But it is not only in the mind of man that this idea of death exists

Questions and Answers, 5th May 1929
There is, for instance, now abroad the beginning of a knowledge among the scientists that death is not a necessity. But the whole of humanity believes firmly in death; it is, one might say, a general human suggestion based on a long unchanging experience. If this belief could be cast out first from the conscious mind, then from the vital nature and the subconscious physical layers, death would no longer be inevitable.

But it is not only in the mind of man that this idea of death exists. The animal creation knew it before him.

Death as a fact has been attached to all life upon earth; but man understands it in a different sense from the meaning Nature originally put into it. In man and in the animals that are nearest to his level, the necessity of death has taken a special form and significance to their consciousness; but the subconscious knowledge in this lower Nature which supports it is a feeling of the necessity of renewal and change and transformation.

It was the conditions of matter upon earth that made death indispensable. The whole sense of the evolution of matter has been a growth from a first state of unconsciousness to an increasing consciousness. And in this process of growth dissolution of forms became an inevitable necessity, as things actually took place. For a fixed form was needed in order that the organised individual consciousness might have a stable support. And yet it is the fixity of the form that made death inevitable. Matter had to assume forms; individualisation and the concrete embodiment of life-forces or consciousness forces were impossible without it, and without these there would have been lacking the first conditions of organised existence on the plane of matter. But a definite and concrete formation contracts the tendency to become at once rigid and hard and petrified. The individual form persisted as a too binding mould; it cannot follow the movements of the forces; it cannot change in harmony with the progressive change in the universal dynamism; it cannot meet continually Nature's demand or keep pace with her; it gets out of the current. At a certain point of this growing disparity and disharmony between the form and the force that presses upon it, a complete dissolution of the form is unavoidable. A new form must be created; a new harmony and parity made possible. This is the true significance of death and this is its use in Nature. But if the form can become more quick and pliant and the cells of the body can be awakened to change with the changing consciousness, there would be no need of a drastic dissolution, death would be no longer inevitable.

All possible things happen, and everything can be done

Is it sure that in the next life too one will be here or in the Ashram? Or will it be that one will go somewhere else for other experiences?

This depends on the cases. First, what do you call the next life? You mean for people who have left their body and will take another?

Yes.

Well, it depends absolutely on the condition in which they died and their last wish, and on the resolution of the psychic. It is not a mechanical or imposed thing, it is different for each one.

I have already told you many times that, for the destiny which follows after death, the last state of consciousness is usually the most important.

That is, if at the moment of death one has the intense aspiration to return to continue his work, then the conditions are arranged for it to be done.

But, you see, there are all the possibilities for what happens after death.

There are people who return in the psychic. You see, I have told you that the outer being is very rarely preserved; so we speak only of the psychic consciousness which, indeed, always persists.

And then there are people for whom the psychic returns to the psychic domain to assimilate the experience they have had and to prepare their future life. This may take centuries, it depends on the people.

The more evolved the psychic is, the nearer it is to its complete maturity, the greater the time between the births. There are beings who reincarnate only after a thousand years, two thousand years.

The closer one is to the beginning of the formation, the closer are the reincarnations; and sometimes even, altogether at the lower level, when man is quite near the animal, it goes like this (*gesture*), that is, it is not unusual for people to reincarnate in the children of their children, like that, something like that, or just in the next generation. But this is always on a very primitive level of evolution, and the psychic being is not very conscious, it is in the state of formation.

And as it becomes more developed, the reincarnations, as I said, are at a greater distance from one another.

When the psychic being is fully developed, when it no longer needs to return to earth for its development, when it is absolutely free, it has the choice between no longer coming back to earth if it finds that its work lies elsewhere or if it prefers to remain in the purely psychic consciousness, without reincarnating; or else it can come when it wants, as it wants, where it wants, perfectly consciously.

And there are those who have united with forces of a universal order and with entities of the Overmind or elsewhere, who remain all the time in the earth atmosphere and take on bodies successively for the work.

This means that the moment the psychic being is completely formed and absolutely free – when it is completely formed it becomes absolutely free – it can do anything it likes, it depends on what it chooses; therefore one can't say, "It will be like this, it will be like that"; it does exactly what it wants and it can even announce (that has happened), at the moment of the death of the body, what its next reincarnation will be and what it will do, and already choose what it is going to do.

But before this state, which is not very frequent – depends absolutely on the degree of development of the psychic and the hope formulated by the integral consciousness of the being – there is still the mental, vital and physical consciousness, united with the psychic consciousness; so at that moment, the moment of death, the moment of leaving the body, it formulates a hope or an aspiration or a will, and usually this decides the future life.

So one can't ask a question saying, "What happens and what should be done?" All possible things happen, and everything can be done.

Everyone has one thing in mind: he asks a general question but in his mind it is an altogether particular question; but this - these things one does not discuss in public.

Questions and Answers, 16th March 1955, pp.85-87

The playground talk of July 1st, 1953

"The human being is at home and safe in the material body; the body is his protection. There are some who are full of contempt for their bodies and think that things will be much better and easier after death without them. But in fact the body is your fortress and your shelter. While you are lodged in it the forces of the hostile world find it difficult to have a direct hold upon you.... Directly you enter any realm of this (vital) world, its beings gather round you to get out of you all you have, to draw what they can and make it a food and a prey. If you have no strong light and force radiating from within you, you move there without your body as if you had no coat to protect you against a chill and bleak atmosphere, no house to shield you, even no skin covering you, your nerves exposed and bare. There are men who say, 'How unhappy I am in this body,' and think of death as an escape! But after death you have the same vital surroundings and are in danger from the same forces that are the cause of your misery in this life....

"It is here upon earth, in the body itself, that you must acquire a complete knowledge and learn to use a full and complete power. Only when you have done that will you be free to move about with entire security in all the worlds."

Questions and Answers 1929, 12th May 1929

(A child) After death people enter the vital world, but those who do good go to paradise?

Where is your paradise? Who has taught you that? They have spoken to you of heaven and hell and purgatory?... No? Not of all that? From where did you gather your idea of paradise? From which book?

I have heard about it.

But from whom?

I do not remember now.

It is generally what religious priests say to the faithful to encourage them to do good. For it is a notorious fact that life is not more easy for the good than for the wicked; usually it is the contrary: the wicked succeed better than the good! So people who are not very spiritual say to themselves: "Why should I take the trouble of being good? It is better to be wicked and have an easy life." It is very difficult to make them understand that there are many kinds of good and that sometimes it is worth the trouble perhaps to make an effort to be good. So to make this intelligible to the least intelligent, they are told: "There, it is very simple. If you are quite obedient, quite nice, quite unselfish, if you always do good deeds, and if you believe in the dogmas we teach, well, when you die, God will send you to Paradise. If you have sometimes good will, sometimes bad, if, sometimes you do good, sometimes you don't, and if you think very much of yourself and very little of others, then when you die, you will be sent to Purgatory for another experience. And then if you are thoroughly wicked, if you are always doing harm to others, doing all kinds of bad things and you do not care about the good of anyone and particularly if you do not believe in the dogma that we teach you, then you will go straight to Hell and for eternity."

This is one of the prettiest inventions I have ever heard of: they have invented eternal hell. That is to say, once you are in hell, it is for eternity.... You understand what that means, for eternity? You will be tortured and burnt (in the hot countries you are burnt, in the cold countries you are frozen), and that for eternity. That is it. So I do not know who taught you those pretty things; but they are simply inventions to make people obey, to keep them under control.

There are teachings which are not like that. There are religions which are not like that. But still one can, in a poetic, picturesque, descriptive manner speak of a paradise; because this paradise means a wonderful place where there is utmost joy and happiness and comfort.... And yet that depends upon the religion to which you belong. For there are heavens where you pass your time singing praises to God, you do nothing else - but in the end that must be somewhat wearisome; however, there you pass your time playing music and singing the praises of God. There are other heavens, on the contrary, where you enjoy all possible pleasures, all that you desired to have during your life, you have in heaven. There are heavens where you are constantly in blissful meditation - but for people who are not keen on meditating, that must be rather tiresome. However, that depends, you know: they have invented all kinds of things so that people may really want to be wise and obey the laws given to them.

And man's imagination is so creative, such a form-maker, that there really are in the world places like these heavens. There are places also like these hells and there are places like these purgatories. Man creates out of nothing the things he imagines. If your consciousness be enlightened, then you can be pulled out of these places; otherwise you are shut up, imprisoned there by the very belief you had when alive. You will tell me that it is equal to a life, but it is an altogether illusory and extremely limited existence. It is real only for those who think like that. As soon as you think differently, it does not exist for you any longer; you can come out of it. You can pull a person out of these places, and immediately he perceives that he was imprisoned in his own formation.

Man has an extraordinary power of creation. He has created a whole set of godheads in his own image, having the same faults as himself, doing on a bigger scale, with greater power whatever he does. These beings have a relative existence, but still it is an independent existence, just like your thought. When you have a thought, a well-made mental formation which goes out of you, it becomes an independent entity and continues on its way and it does that for which it was made. It continues to act independently of you. That is why you must be on your guard. If you have made such a formation and it has gone out, it has gone out to do its work; and after a time you find out that it was perhaps not a very happy thing to have a thought like that, that this formation was not very beneficial; now that it has gone out, it is very difficult for you to get hold of it again. You must have considerable occult knowledge. It has gone out and is moving on its way.... Supposing in a moment of great anger (I do not say that you do so, but still) when you were in quite a rage against someone, you said: "Ah! Couldn't some misfortune befall him?" Your formation has gone on its way. It has gone out and you have no longer any control over it; and it goes and organises some misfortune or other: it is going to do its work. And after some time the misfortune arrives. Happily, you do not usually have sufficient knowledge to tell yourself: "Oh! It is I who am responsible," but that is the truth.

Note that this power of formation has a great advantage, if one knows how to use it. You can make good formations and if you make them properly, they will act in the same way as the others. You can do a lot of good to people just by sitting quietly in your room, perhaps even more good than by undergoing a lot of trouble externally. If you know how to think correctly, with force and intelligence and kindness, it you love someone and wish him well very sincerely, deeply, with all your heart, that does him much good, much more certainly than you think. I have said this often; for example, to those who are here, who learn that someone in their family is very ill and feel that childish impulse of wanting to rush immediately to the spot to attend to the sick person. I tell you, unless it is an exceptional case and there is nobody to attend on the sick person (and at times even in such a case), if you know how to keep the right attitude and concentrate with affection and good will upon the sick person, if you know how to pray for him and make helpful formations, you will do him much more good than if you go to nurse him, feed him, help him wash himself, indeed all that everybody can do. Anybody can nurse a person. But not everybody can make good formations and send out forces that act for healing.

In any case, to come back to our paradise, it is a childish deformation - ignorant or political - of something which is true in a sense but not quite like that.... I have told you many times and I could not repeat it too often, that one is not built up of one single piece. We have within us many states of being and each state of being has its own life. All this is put together in one single body, so long as you have a body, and acts through that single body; so that gives you the feeling that it is one single person, a single being. But there are many beings and particularly there are concentrations on different levels: just as you have a physical being, you have a vital being, you have a mental being, you have a psychic being, you have many others and all possible intermediaries. But it is a little complicated, you might not understand. Suppose you were living a life of desire, passion and impulse: you live with your vital being dominant in you; but if you live with spiritual effort, with great good will, the desire to do things well and an unselfishness, a will for progress, you live with the psychic being dominant in you.

Then, when you are about to leave your body, all these beings start to disperse.

Only if you are a very advanced yogi and have been able to unify your being around the divine centre, do these beings remain bound together. If you have not known how to unify yourself, then at the time of death all that is dispersed: each one returns to its domain.

For example, with regard to the vital being, all your different desires will be separated and each one run towards its own realisation, quite independently, for the physical being will no longer be there to hold them together.

But if you have united your consciousness with the psychic consciousness, when you die you remain conscious of your psychic being and the psychic being returns to the psychic world, which is a world of bliss and delight and peace and tranquillity and of a growing knowledge. So, if you like to call that a paradise, it is all right; because in fact, to the extent to which you are identified with your psychic being, you remain conscious of it, you are one with it, and it is immortal and goes to its immortal domain to enjoy a perfectly happy life or rest. If you like to call that paradise, call it paradise. If you are good, if you have become conscious of your psychic and live in it, well, when your body dies, you will go with your psychic being to take rest in the psychic world, in a blissful state.

But if you have lived in your vital with all its impulses, each impulse will try to realise itself here and there... For example, a miser who is concentrated upon his money, when he dies, the part of the vital that was interested in his money will be stuck there and will continue to watch over the money so that nobody may take it. People do not see him, but he is there all the same, and is very unhappy if something happens to his precious money. I knew quite well a lady who had a good amount of money and children; she had five children who were all prodigals, each one more than the other. The same amount of care she had taken in amassing the money, they seemed to take in squandering it; they spent it at random. So when the poor old lady died, she came to see me and told me: "Ah, now they are going to squander my money!" And she was extremely unhappy. I consoled her a little, but I had a good deal of difficulty in persuading her not to keep watching over her money so that it might not be wasted.

Now, if you live exclusively in your physical consciousness (it is difficult, for you have, after all, thoughts and feelings, but if you live exclusively in your physical), when the physical being disappears, you disappear at the same time, it is finished.... There is a spirit of the form: your form has a spirit which persists for seven days after your death. The doctors have declared that you are dead, but the spirit of your form lives, and not only does it live but it is conscious in most of the cases. But that lasts for seven or eight days and afterwards it is dissolved. I am not speaking of yogis; I am speaking of ordinary people. Yogis have no laws, it is quite different; for them the world is different. I am speaking to you of ordinary men living an ordinary life; for these it is like that.

So the conclusion is that if you want to preserve your consciousness, it would be better to centralise it on a part of your being that is immortal; otherwise it will vanish like a flame in the air. And it is very fortunate, for if it were otherwise, there would be perhaps gods or types of superior men who would create hells and heavens as they do in their material imagination, where they would imprison you; you would be imprisoned in heaven or in hell according as you pleased or displeased them. It would be a very critical situation and happily it is not like that.

It is said that there is a god of Death. Is it true?

Yes, I call it the spirit of Death. I know it very well. And that is an extraordinary organisation. You do not know to what an extent it is organised.

I believe there are many of these spirits of death, I believe there are hundreds. I have met at least two of them. One I met in France and the other in Japan, and they were very different; which leads one to believe that probably in accordance with the mental culture, the education, the country and beliefs there should be different spirits. But there are spirits of all the manifestations of Nature: there are spirits of fire, spirits of air, of water, of rain, of wind; and there are spirits of death.

Each spirit of death, whatever it may be, has a claim to a certain number of deaths per day. Indeed, it is a kind of alliance between the vital forces and the forces of Nature. For example, if the spirit of death has decided: "That is the number of people to which I am entitled," let us say four or five or six, or one or two persons, it depends on the day; it has decided that certain persons would die, it goes straight and settles down beside the person about to die. But if you happen to be conscious (not the person), if you see the spirit going to a person and you do not want him to die, then you can, if you possess a certain occult power, tell it: "No, I forbid you to take him." It is a thing that has happened, not once but several times, in Japan and here. It was not the same spirit. That is what makes me say that there must be many.

— I don't want him to die.

— But I have a right to one death!

— Go and find someone who is ready to die.

So I have seen several cases: sometimes it is just a neighbour who dies suddenly in place of the other, sometimes it is an acquaintance and sometimes it is an enemy. Naturally, there is a relation, good or bad, of neighbourhood (or anything else) which externally looks like chance. But it is the spirit who has taken its dead. The spirit has a claim to one death, it will have one death. You can tell it: "I forbid you to take this one," and have the power of sending it away, and the spirit can do nothing but go away; but it does not give up its due and goes elsewhere. There is another death.

It is the same thing with fire. I saw the spirit of fire, particularly in Japan because fire is an extraordinary thing in that country. When a fire starts, some eighty houses burn: a whole quarter. It is something fantastic. The houses are of wood and they burn like match-boxes; you see a fire kindling and then all of a sudden, puff!... You have never seen a match-box catching fire? A flash! Like that, a flash! One, two, three, ten, twenty houses burnt down before my eyes!... So there are spirits of fire. One day, I was in my bed. I was concentrating, looking at people. Suddenly I saw something like a cloud of flames drawing close to the house. I looked and I saw it was a conscious being.

— Eh! What are you here for?

— I have the right to burn the house, start a fire.

— That's possible, I told it, but not here.

And it could not resist.

It is a question of who proves the stronger. I said: "No, here you can't burn, that's all!" Five minutes later I heard cries:

"Ah! Ah!" Two or three houses farther away, a house had caught fire. It had gone there as I had forbidden it to come to my house. It had a claim to one house. There we are!

Sometimes when people are dying, they know that they are about to die. Why don't they tell the spirit to go away?

Ah! Well, that depends upon the people. Two things are necessary. First of all, nothing in your being, no part of your being should want to die. That does not happen often. You have always a defeatist in you somewhere: something that is tired, something that is disgusted, something that has had enough of it, something that is lazy, something that does not want to struggle and says: "Well! Ah! Let it be finished, so much the better." That is sufficient, you are dead.

But it is a fact: if nothing, absolutely nothing in you consents to die, you will not die. For someone to die, there is always a second, perhaps the hundredth part of a second, when he gives his consent. If there is not this second of consent, he does not die.

I knew people who should have really died according to all physical and vital laws; and they refused. They said: "No, I will not die," and they lived. There are others who do not need at all to die, but they are of that kind and say: "Ah! Well! Yes, so much the better, it will be finished," and it is finished. Even that much, even nothing more than that: you need not have a persistent wish, you have only to say: "Well, yes, I have had enough!" and it is finished. So it is truly like that. As you say, you may have death standing by your bedside and tell him: "I do not want you, go away," and it will be obliged to go away. But usually one gives way, for one must struggle, one must be strong, one must be very courageous and enduring, must have a great faith in the necessity of life; like someone, for example, who feels very strongly that he has still something to do and he must absolutely do it. But who is sure he has not within him the least bit of a defeatist, somewhere, who just yields and says: "It is all right"!... It is here, the necessity of unifying oneself.

Whatever the way we follow, the subject we study, we always arrive at the same result. The most important thing for an individual is to unify himself around his divine centre; in that way he becomes a true individual, master of himself and his destiny. Otherwise, he is a plaything of forces that toss him about like a piece of cork on a river. He goes where he does not want to go, he is made to do things he does not want to do, and finally he loses himself in a hole without having any strength to recover. But if you are consciously organised, unified around the divine centre, ruled and directed by it, you are master of your destiny. That is worth the trouble of attempting.... In any case, I find it preferable to be the master rather than the slave. It is a rather unpleasant sensation to feel yourself pulled by the strings and made to do things whether you want to or not - that is quite irrelevant - but to be compelled to act because something pulls you by the strings, something which you do not even see - that is exasperating. However, I do not know, but I found it very exasperating, even when I was quite a child. At five, it began to seem to me quite intolerable and I sought for a way so that it might be otherwise - without people getting a chance to scold me. For I knew nobody who could help me and I did not have the chance that you have, someone who can tell you: "This is what you have to do!" There was nobody to tell me that. I had to find it out all by myself. And I found it. I started at five. And you, you were five long ago....

Voilà.

Four conversations of the Mother

May 17th, 1969

You know that I used to see Pavitra every day, in the evening. He was in a poor state. But I had been forewarned ago that his inner being was waiting for X to return before it would leave. I don't know whether he was aware of something in his outward consciousness, but at any rate he had never said anything. But I knew … The day X arrived, that very day (*May 31st*), just before coming here, Pavitra fell down. He came here with quite a few scratches. I thought it would stop there, but the day after X's arrival (*I don't remember, I never have a clear memory of dates*), at any rate between the 15th and 16th, at night, after 9 (*I didn't look at the time, so I don't know precisely, but I was on my bed*), Pavitra's whole individualised consciousness (*but not in a form*), his conscious, fully awakened consciousness, down to all that can come out of the cells, began to come and enter into me according to the ancient, the very old yogic practice of merging into the Supreme – in that way, that very process. It happened while I was lying on my bed; it began, and it was so material that there was a very strong friction in all the cells, everywhere. And it lasted for three hours. After three hours, it became … not exactly still, but no longer active. Then, the next morning, I saw X (*it was on the 16th*), I saw X at about 8:30 (*naturally, Pavitra had been in bed since the day before, they had put him to bed*), and in the morning, X told me that just as he was about to come here, Pavitra opened his eyes and looked at him … So I told him, "I don't know, but with a yogic knowledge of the process, quite an extraordinary knowledge (*because he had never boasted of having it*), his conscious being melted last night and entered my body, this body…" I told him, "We'll see." But half an hour later, they told me that just as I was talking with X, the doctor declared that he had left.

Have you seen him? I am told he looks very good.

Oh, Yes!

I had first said that he would be buried this morning at 10 o'clock, since the end came even before the doctors declared it was over, but I had it delayed until 4 ... I can't say that he has remained separate *(from Mother)*, not at all, but from time to time ... there's his way of reacting to something; it's quite interesting. And he has brought with him an extraordinary sense of satisfaction! As if, "Ah, at last..." Like that. And it's constant, night and day. I wanted to see at night whether something of him would still come, but it was all over, there was nothing more... It was done as a super-yogi might do it! He'd never boasted about it, I don't even know whether he actively knew it. He did it wonderfully. You know, the stories that are told of those who shut themselves in a cave and who would leave like that – that's it.

They didn't exactly lift him up, because he hadn't fallen down, but they found him standing, unable to move. It was after lunch (on the 15th he had lunch with X), and immediately after lunch, he asked X to leave, and wanted to go to his terrace – it took an hour to get there! It's while coming back from there that he remained like that, standing – he nearly fell down, so he had to be carried to his bed (that is to say, in the afternoon of the 15th), and it was during the night that he did that. So then, I had said he would be buried this morning, that is on the 17th, then X came and told me he was quite intact, there was no stiffening (he had gone to see him with Y, who is a doctor, and Y said that was because Pavitra was so thin), so I said we might as well wait till this afternoon. It has been postponed till 4 o'clock. But as for me, last night I looked carefully: there's nothing. Even if there is something, a little consciousness left, to let him go.

But I wasn't expecting it, I wasn't thinking about it, didn't even know that he knew how to go out like that – it must have been something deep within him that knew it. I didn't even know he knew how to do it. Because the evening before Pavitra left, I told X (X had told me what happened at lunch time), I told him, "Generally, I don't see Pavitra, it's very rare, very rare, it happens quite accidentally, and it's more symbolic visions than..." I said to him, "I don't see him, I don't know, but this night, of the 15th, that is, I'll inquire to see what it is, in what state he is, and see if he goes out of his body or comes to me."

There was nothing in a form, nothing. And some time after I'd lain down, it started coming, but then with an extraordinary *science* of the process! And for *three* hours without stop, continuously, in the most *steady* manner, like that: an action. After three hours, it was as it is now; I felt as if he said, "Now it's over." Only, one never knows, isn't it, if there was some consciousness lingering in the body... I thought it would be better to wait till this afternoon, not to shut him up with something in his body.

It has brought to the body consciousness a sort of sense of satisfaction: the appeasement that satisfaction gives. And that quite concretely.

Did he know it from a previous life, or...? I don't know. Or else, he just didn't talk about it. Because the way he spoke, he didn't seem to know the secrets of yogic processes. It was done with a rare perfection ... Three hours, without stop, without flagging – three hours – continuous, continuous.

Silence

When Sri Aurobindo left, I was standing near his bed (later on, when he was alone, when there was no one), and all the Supramental force he had concentrated in his body (what was left in his body), he passed it on to me. I was standing near his bed; he had been declared "dead", but all that Supramental consciousness which was there came out of his body, slowly, and directly entered into mine. It was so material that I felt the friction of the force everywhere, all over. But it was slightly luminous. That was something different than with Pavitra. As for Sri Aurobindo, he... (how can I put it?), he stayed mainly ... I found him everywhere: I found him all the way up, absolutely one with the Supreme Consciousness; I found him having spread out and being in many places to see many people and do a lot of work; and I found him (but then, in a precise form, though *not fixed* – a precise, rather supple form that looked like him, like what we knew of him, with more suppleness, without the fixity of the physical, but quite precise, a form in his likeness, absolutely in his likeness), in the subtle physical. There he has a dwelling, he is settled and he remains there permanently (which doesn't prevent him from being at many other places and...), but there, there is a Sri Aurobindo whom I see almost every night, who looks after the whole work, who sees people, and who is almost constantly with me. In the subtle physical, it's a specific place, and very large – huge, you know – he is there, seeing people, doing all kinds of things...

Apart from that, in Amrita's[1] case, it was something different again. Amrita used to come in spite of his illness, he used to come and see me every day; he would come upstairs in the morning and sit down here, and once again in the evening (you have seen how much work it was to climb the stairs). In his case, when he left ... The doctor had told him, "You can't go upstairs for a month," and it's after that, later on that day, that he came: he didn't accept, he left his body and came – he came straight to me. But he was *in his own form*, more subtle, but precisely defined *(Mother draws an outline showing Amrita's form)*, it was his form, in his likeness. And he remained there, now active and now at rest (he rests more than he is active, but now and then he is still active). It's like ... like a shadow, you understand, which is wholly in my atmosphere. And he has remained there – he remains there, rests there. But in Pavitra's case, it was something else altogether: it's the entire conscious being which gave up... (how can I put it?) its limits, the personal limit and form, so as to identify totally – he entered like that, like a stream of consciousness and force, but

---

1. Amrita left his body on 31 January 1969.

very material, very material: it produced a friction, I felt a friction, and for three hours. I had never seen that before, it was the first time – I had heard about it very often (it's often mentioned), how the great yogis knew how to do it: they would go like that, deliberately.

And it has *added* something to the body consciousness. In the body's spontaneous attitude, its way of being, I have noticed a slight change; it has added a sort of ... stability in the body: a satisfied stability, like that. It's not like something that comes and might go, it's not that: it's here *(in Mother)*. It has been really quite interesting – and unexpected.

I wanted to be sure that there was nothing left that could make the body suffer, but now I think it's over.

Does it mean that his individuality has been dissolved?

These notions of individuality, you know ... for me, they've changed a lot, quite a lot. This whole morning again... But for a long time, at least for a month, it is something else.

When people speak of individuality, there's always a sort of ... at least a background of separation, that is, something that exists independently and has its own destiny. Now, as the consciousness in the body knows it, it's almost like a pulsation of "something" which *momentarily* has a separate action, but which, deeply, essentially, is always one; like something projected like this *(gesture of expansion)*, momentarily with a form, and then ... *(gesture of contraction)* it can cancel that form at will. It's very hard to explain, but at any rate, the sense of the permanence of separation has completely disappeared; completely. The universe is an exteriorisation *(same gesture of pulsation)* of the Supreme Consciousness; it's our incapacity of total vision that enables us to have that sense of fixity: there is none, it's something like pulsations or ... really a play of forms – there is only *one* being. There is only one being. There is only one, only one Consciousness, only one Being.

Separation is really ... I don't know what happened... And that's what made all the mischief – all the misfortune, all the misery ... For the last few days, this body has gone through a series of experiences (it would be much too long to tell), through all the states of consciousness one can go through, from the sense of the single reality of this *(Mother pinches the skin of her hands)*, of the substance, with all the misery, all the suffering which is the consequence of seeing matter as the single reality – from that to liberation. Hour after hour, it has been a whole work. And this incident of Pavitra's departure has come as an example, as a demonstration.

But even before that, the consciousness of the cells had realised the oneness – the true, essential oneness which *can* become total ... if this sort of illusion disappears. You understand, the illusion which has created all this misery was lived so intensely that it became almost unbearable, with all the horrors and all the terrors it has created in the human consciousness and on the earth... There have been dreadful things. And just after that – just after: liberation.

What remains to be lived, that is, the experience that remains to be had, is ... the next progress of the creation, of matter – the next step to return to the true Consciousness. That's...

It seems to have been decided that something like a beginning, or an attempt of experience, is going to be made *(Mother touches her body)*. It's a question of intensity of faith, or of the power to bear that faith gives. All depends on the capacity to go through the necessary experiences.

In any case, all the old notions, all the old ways of understanding things, all that is quite over, it's past.

And all that is necessarily the return path; we had to go through the path and we still have to go through it (though not the same thing), but all the while progressing until we can ... until this *(the body)* is ready to live the Truth. I don't know, the impression is that things are going as fast as they can possibly go; the Consciousness is really making us move forward as fast as possible. It's no longer the time of a drowsiness that drags on.

Long silence

I can say (and it was almost like a surprise, I mean I didn't know it), I can say that the consciousness that came out of Pavitra's body was a consciousness without ego – without ego. Without the *sense* of ego. There was a clear will to merge, a will with an intensity of aspiration, it was fantastic! Fantastic.

But by individuality, I don't mean an ego: I mean the "something" that's identical through all lives, the one thing that progresses through all lives. The "something" that remains the same and pursues its development.

That's the Supreme.

Yes, but there is something that...

It's the Supreme conscious of Himself...

Yes.

... partially.

Yes, that's it, there is something...

The Supreme partially conscious of Himself.

... that pursues a line of development.

Yes, that's the process. It's the process that has been used for evolution.

Yes, that's what I call individuality.

That's agreed. It's the process, it has been the process of the creation.
And it's because it was the process of the creation that men have confused it with...

Separation.

With separation: the ego.

But that (*the "something" that persists*) is obvious. It's there, very strong, in this action of Pavitra's – it was very strong. And in fact, it was free from the illusion of ego and had the full force of That. But that (*the centre*) remains! It can't disappear.

Silence

What's going to happen? I don't know.

Because it (*this merging of Pavitra*) is very clearly part of the work: there are no accidents, nothing, nothing of the sort (all that has vanished), everything very clearly happened exactly as it had to happen. It seems to mean that "one" is attempting something (*Mother touches her body*). But what? I don't know... The body isn't at all worried, it's like this (*Mother opens her hands*); always this: "What You will, Lord, what You will..." And with a smile and perfect joy – this way, that way, that other way ... (*fluid gesture, as if to indicate this or that side of the world, or all kinds of other sides*)... Very strangely, it has been given a consciousness that no longer has anything to do with time: you understand, there isn't "when it was not," there isn't "when it will no longer be," there isn't ... It's not like that, everything is something in motion. But it's really very interesting. And all, all those reactions, those sensations, those feelings, all that has completely changed – changed even in their appearance. It's something else.

You understand, the states one could be in when one was in the highest consciousnesses – those that were united, were automatically one with the Supreme Consciousness and were conscious of the whole – those states have become the body's natural state. Effortlessly, spontaneously: it cannot be otherwise. So what's going to happen? How is it going to take expression? I don't know...

It's contrary to all habits.

80

Does this consciousness know what needs to be done on the material level? I don't know. But the body doesn't worry about that at all, it does what it has to do from second to second, without asking any questions. No complications, no plans, nothing, nothing.

There.

We'll see, it's interesting!

—

May 21st, 1969

(Regarding some photographs that were taken just before Pavitra's coffin was closed and lowered into the ground.)

I saw the photos – have you seen them? Have you been shown the photos? They took some there. I am telling you about it because there was something interesting. There was a photo with you there (there was X, there was the governor, there was...), just when you were all lowering the coffin. And then... (you know, this presence of Pavitra hasn't merged with the rest [*of Mother*]: it has remained there very peacefully, he is very peaceful – it hasn't merged), and then, just as I looked at the photo and saw you, there was something like this within *(gesture to the heart, like an emotion)*, I don't know, it was almost like a tenderness, and he was almost happy. I can't explain what it is, he was like this: "Oh! Satprem..."

He was really very pleased.

It's curious. I wasn't expecting it: I was given the photos and started looking at them, when I suddenly felt something *(same gesture to the heart...)*. It struck me very much. Because you had asked me, "Is he going to merge?" So even that, even that contact he has kept. Now and then, when someone says something regarding the work, he has his remark to make (I've noticed that), but there, it was very strong, almost like an "Oh!" of joy, you understand: "Oh! Satprem." So I thought, "It's good, since it really pleased him."

I am wondering whether the consciousness (of Pavitra) has been especially preserved intact because it entered here (into Mother), or whether it's always like that? ... Where does someone conscious go? Does he remain here? ... I told you, with Amrita, it's a sort of not too precise form; it's always there, now resting, now waking up, but he doesn't seem to be particularly interested in material things. While Pavitra, from what I see, seems to be conscious of them. It's something rather remarkable, I think.

I have seen cases of people who took interest and continued to take interest in what goes on (*here*), but then they have an independent form. While with Pavitra, it's something else.

It struck me because it was strong, like this (*same gesture to the heart*).

All these last few weeks, there has been a sort of constant ... I can't call it "preoccupation", but a sort of need to know: to what extent and how do those who have left remain conscious of the things they used to do, for instance, take interest in them, look after them (supposing they have the means to do so)?

A case such as Sri Aurobindo's is quite different: it's as if he had been multiplied. He has a constant presence in the subtle physical: he goes about, visits a number of people, and he is conscious of a lot of things, he intervenes in a lot of things, but a considerable number – it has multiplied his action. But that's exceptional.

Silence

I have often wondered about the same thing. I've often asked myself whether on the other side I'll be as unconscious of this side as I am here unconscious of the other side!

Mother laughs heartily

Most people – the vast majority of people – go into a sort of assimilative sleep: all the experiences they had in their lives, all they learned, the consciousness seems to ruminate over that.

In the beginning ... (Théon knew a lot of things – I don't know how he came to know them, but I verified them and found them to be correct), in the beginning, the span of time between two lives is very long, and it's a sort of assimilative sleep in which the consequences of what one has learned develop inwardly. Then, as the psychic being is formed and as one grows more conscious, rebirths take place more and more closely, until the time when rebirth becomes the result of a choice: at a precise place, for a specific length of time. And then, depending on what the psychic being wants to do, depending on the action it has to do, the new birth may be near or distant. There, we have all possible differences. But in the formative stage, that's how it is: very distant rebirths. So then, I've often wondered ... You see, Théon says there is a psychic state in which those beings rest (it's true, there is such a place, I know it), but many people, especially at the beginning of their evolution, are quite tied down to the earth; I have seen quite a few people in trees, for instance. Very often I saw them in trees; often, while following someone (*with the inner vision*), I saw him enter into a tree; and often, while looking at a tree, I saw someone in it. I saw others who were ... oh, people clinging to a place they were interested in: for instance, I saw a man who was interested in nothing but his money, which he had hidden somewhere, and as soon as he left his body, he went there, settled there, and refused to budge from there! ... Incidentally (*laughing*), it had a curious result: it led people to discover the place! You see, it caused movements of forces, and some people felt it and thought, "Oh, there must be something here."

There was a time when I concerned myself with that a good deal, and I made a good number of discoveries (following Théon's indications); later on, it no longer interested me. And now, quite lately, I have been reviewing all kinds of things, all kinds of things...

But Pavitra's case, I really believe it's exceptional. It's the first time it has happened to me – with nobody, nobody else before. I told you, when Sri Aurobindo left, for hours he passed on to me the whole Supramental force and consciousness he had concentrated in his body. It was immediately after he left. I felt he had called me; I stood there, near his bed, looking at him, and ... I saw it, you understand: he passed on to me the force, the whole Supramental force he had concentrated in his body, and I felt him everywhere enter like that, with a friction. It lasted for hours. But that's quite an exceptional case, as I told you. But what took place with Pavitra is really ... it's really ... It's not the same thing: he simply came out of his body deliberately (and not his psychic being: it was as material as he could), and I felt him, felt it enter and enter everywhere, all over my body ... And now, if I look within, I can't say I see a form, but ... it's not completely fused. And for certain things – certain things that have to do with people, or the School – there's a very clear personal reaction. And then, those photos ... I think that's quite exceptional.

I felt something in the brain. You know that since Sri Aurobindo gave me mental silence, it has been absolutely still; it never started up again as before, and the consciousness has been there (*gesture above Mother*), working from there. But then after Pavitra came here, something (*gesture to the forehead*) impelled me to ask (I asked what's here, within), "Could I get the mathematical knowledge you had?" I asked him that. And his answer was, "Of course, it would be easy if you set this in motion again!" But that I don't want to do. Anyway...

Anyway, that's how it is, as if I were talking to someone within! How happy he was! I think he loved you very much. He never spoke a word about all that. It has pleased him a lot.

At any rate, with this departure of Pavitra, one thing has been categorical: if there was in the body the least fear of death, or anxiety, it's com-plete-ly gone. With Pavitra's case, it's completely gone, completely. The impression is: "But ... but why do people make such a fuss about that!"

There. It's strange.

May 28th, 1969

They've found in Pavitra's things the record of an experience he had three years ago, just when his cancer was beginning. Would you be interested to know the text of that experience?...

Is it interesting? . . .

Yes.

But anyway...
Pavitra has remained here, not at all mingled; now and then, wholly conscious, otherwise very tranquil. It's good – not a hindrance, you understand... Now and then, he manifests something, which shows he remains conscious. That's all.
As for me, I am continuing .... it's not easy. That's all. So I can listen to this.

(Satprem reads out)

**Pavitra's experience
Night of February 5th, 1966**

It was a night of fully conscious spiritual experience, a night of torture and glory.

I walked through large rooms in which beings without communication with outside were living. And other rooms where wretched beings were dragging out a wretched life. They took notice of my presence, which seemed to bring them a ray of light from outside. A few reacted well, with a smile; others fled. A few knocked against me. Then I went into other rooms. The same goal always seemed to justify my presence. For, as I went by, a few showed a sign of hope. But at the same time obstacles, sufferings, tortures of all kinds fell on me. They were not deliberately inflicted tortures, but sorts of reactions of ignorance and suffering.

This work progressively became more and more difficult for me. I moved about with difficulty, walked more and more slowly, as though overburdened, until it finally became difficult for me to find my way ... to escape.

These experiences seemed to last for a long time. When they ended, I found myself in my physical body, surprised that it bore no marks of all that I had just undergone.

But I slowly began to understand the meaning of all that had taken place. An immense gratitude rose from my heart towards the Supreme, as did an entire self-giving so that His Will may be accomplished everywhere.

I perceived the meaning of the great promise:

"I shall deliver you from all evil, fear not."

That promise of victory from the Divine embodied on the earth carried me away with joy.

I repeat that I was fully conscious for as long as those experiences lasted.

That is all I have to say.

Is it after this that he fell ill?

It's about that time. That's when he started walking with two canes.

After a long silence

It would mean that he took upon himself quite a few people's burdens ... So that would explain what happened: on the day he left, a number of people were terribly attacked by things, as if those were coming back onto them; things that had been taken away from them and which were coming back onto them – specially women.

Long silence

There was in him a being more conscious than him. That's obvious. It was that same being which absorbed (*others' suffering*).

———

September 14th, 1971

(A disciple had gone to the Cazanove Gardens, in the suburbs of Pondicherry, to see the tombstones of Pavitra and Amrita.)

Yesterday I went to visit Cazanove.

Oh, why?

To see Amrita-da and Pavitra-da....

How are they?

They are covered with "Sri Aurobindo's Compassion", and near the head, there is a slightly broken pot with "New Creation", and near the feet a pot of "Devotion", the same for both. ... I found that very nice, but nothing has been done.

I've never heard Pavitra complain about it! (*laughter*) I see Pavitra very often, almost every night. Maybe he likes it that way. Even last night I saw him: he was in Japan. When did they leave?

Arnrita-da left on January 31st, 1969 and Pavitra-da in May, May 16th.

Oh, Pavitra left after.

You know, time and me...

Pavitra is here, he's very active, he stays near me, I see him very often. Amrita I don't see that much. Pavitra was absorbed into me and I put him back into a form little by little, and when he was completely formed, I brought him out and he stays very close here.

What does he do?

He meets people, he does all sorts of things.

What work does he do?

He meets people, talks, but he's here, he hasn't left the earth's atmosphere. Amrita left to rest; Pavitra is here, in the subtle physical – that's where Sri Aurobindo is and it's a physical that has a strong tendency to materialise. We'll see.

(Note: The first three conversations were with Satprem, the fourth with Sujata).

Mother India, 24th April 2012

Overcoming Fear of Death

First Method
The first method appeals to the reason. One can say that in the present state of the world, death is inevitable; a body that has taken birth will necessarily die one day or another. Reason teaches us that it is absurd to fear something that one cannot avoid. The only thing to do is to accept the idea of death and quietly do the best one can from day to day, from hour to hour, without worrying about what is going to happen.

Second Method
Beyond all the emotions, in the silent and tranquil depths of our being, there is a light shining constantly, the light of the psychic consciousness. Go in search of this light, concentrate on it; it is within you. With a persevering will you are sure to find it, and as soon as you enter into it you awake to the sense of immortality.

Third Method
The third method is for those who have faith in a God, their God, and who have given themselves to him ... They have the constant experience of lying at the feet of their Beloved in an absolute self-surrender or of being cradled in his arms and enjoying a perfect security. There is no longer any room in their consciousness for fear, anxiety or torment; all that has been replaced by a calm and delightful bliss.

Fourth Method
Finally there are those who are born warriors. They cannot accept life as it is and they feel pulsating within them their right to immortality, an integral and earthly immortality. They possess a kind of intuitive knowledge that death is nothing but a bad habit; they seem to be born with the resolution to conquer it.

Yet another Method
There is yet another way ... It is to enter into the domain of death deliberately and consciously while one is still alive, and then to return from this region and to re-enter the physical body, resuming the course of material existence with full knowledge. But for that one must be an initiate.

Attitude towards the Departed

Sweet Mother,
How should the news of death be received, especially when it is someone close to us?

Say to the Supreme Lord: "Let Thy Will be done", and remain as peaceful as possible.

If the departed one is a person one loves, one should concentrate one's love on him in peace and calm, for that is what can most help the one who has departed.

To commit suicide is the most foolish action that a man can do ...

Know for certain that to commit suicide is the most foolish action that a man can do ... what was troubling you while you were alive continues to trouble you when you are dead, without the possibility of diverting your mind which you can get when you are alive.

Suicide, far from being a solution, is a stupid aggravation of the situation, that for perhaps centuries will make life intolerable.

In the Ramayana: Mass Suicide?

The Ramayana says that when Rama saw that his work on earth was finished, he entered the river Sarayu along with his companions. This looks like mass suicide and suicide is regarded as the greatest sin. How to understand this?

1. For the Supreme there is no sin.
2. For the devotee there is no greater sin than to be far from the Lord.
3. At the time when the Ramayana was conceived and written, the knowledge revealed by Sri Aurobindo that the earth will be transformed into a divine world and an abode of the Supreme was not known or accepted.

If you consider these three points you will understand the legend. (Although it may be that the actual facts were not as they have been told.)

The Mother, Felicity Eternal, p.88: M12: 83; M12: 84; M12: 87

The movement of the psychic being dropping the outer sheaths on its way to the psychic plane is the normal movement.

But there can be any number of variations; one can return from the vital plane and there are many cases of an almost immediate birth, sometimes even attended with a complete memory of the events of the past life.

Hell and heaven are often imaginary states of the soul or rather of the vital which it constructs about it after its passing. What is meant by hell is a painful passage through the vital or lingering there, as for instance, in many cases of suicide where one remains surrounded by the forces of suffering and turmoil created by this unnatural and violent exit. There are, of course, also worlds of mind and vital worlds which are penetrated with joyful or dark experiences. One may pass through these as the result of things formed in the nature which create the necessary affinities, but the idea of reward or retribution is a crude and vulgar conception which is a mere popular error.

There is no rule of complete forgetfulness in the return of the soul to rebirth. There are, especially in childhood, many impressions of the past life which can be strong and vivid enough, but the materialising education and influence of the environments prevent their true nature from being recognised. There are even a great number of people who have definite recollections of a past life. But these things are discouraged by education and the atmosphere and cannot remain or develop; in most cases they are stifled out of existence. At the same time it must be noted that what the psychic being carries away with it and brings back is ordinarily the essence of the experiences it had in former lives, and not the details, so that you cannot expect the same memory as one has of the present existence.

A soul can go straight to the psychic world but it depends on the state of consciousness at the time of departure. If the psychic is in front at the time, the immediate transition is quite possible. It does not depend on the acquisition of a mental and vital as well as a psychic immortality - those who have acquired that would rather have the power to move about in the different worlds and even act on the physical world without being bound to it. On the whole, it may be said that there is no one rigid rule for these things, manifold variations are possible depending upon the consciousness, its energies, tendencies and formations, although there is a general framework and design into which all fit and take their place.

If one is in a body with an inadequate will or some distortion in the thought, or an egoism too ... too hardened, and it ends in suicide, it is dreadful.

This is how it works: the psychic being passes from one life to another, but there are cases in which the psychic incarnates in order to ... to work out ... to pass through a certain experience, to learn a certain thing, to develop a certain thing through a certain experience. And so in this life, in the life where the experience is to be made, it can happen (there may be more than one reason) that the soul does not come down accurately in the place it should have, some shift or other may occur, a set of contrary circumstances – this happens sometimes – and then the incarnation miscarries entirely and the soul leaves. But in other cases, the soul is simply placed in the impossibility of doing exactly what it wants and it finds itself swept away by ... unfortunate circumstances. Not only unfortunate from an objective standpoint, but unfortunate for its own development, and then that creates in it the necessity to begin the experience all over again, and in much more difficult conditions.

And if – it can happen – if the second attempt also miscarries, if the conditions make the experience the soul is seeking still more difficult ... for example, if one is in a body with an inadequate will or some distortion in the thought, or an egoism too ... too hardened, and it ends in suicide, it is dreadful. I have seen this many times, it creates a dreadful karma that can be repeated for lifetimes on end before the soul can conquer it and manage to do what it wants. And each time, the conditions become more difficult, each time it requires a still greater effort. And people who know this say, 'You cannot get out!' In fact, it is this kind of desire to escape which pushes you into more foolish things that result in a still greater accumulation of difficulty. There are moments – moments and circumstances – when no one is there to help you, and then things become so ... horrible, the circumstances become so abominable.

Mother specified: 'The subconscious memory of the past creates a kind of irresistible desire to escape from the difficulty, and you recommence the same foolishness, or an even greater foolishness.'

But if the soul has had but ONE call, but ONE contact with the Grace, then in your next life you are put in the conditions, once, whereby EVERYTHING can be swept away at one stroke. And at this present moment on earth, you cannot imagine the number of people I have met – that is, the number of souls – who had reached out towards this possibility with such an intensity – and they have all found themselves on my path.

At that point, sometimes a great courage is needed, sometimes a great endurance is needed, sometimes a true love is enough, sometimes, oh! if only faith were there, one thing, one tiny little thing is enough, and ... everything can be swept away. I have done it often; there are times when I have failed. But more often than not I have been able to remove it. But then, what is needed is a great, stoical courage or a capacity to endure and to SEE IT THROUGH. The resistance (especially in cases of former suicide), the resistance to the temptation of renewing this stupidity creates a terrible formation. Or else this habit of fleeing when suffering comes: flee, flee, instead of ... absorbing the difficulty, holding on.

But just this, a faith in the Grace, or an awareness of the Grace, or the intensity of the call, or else naturally the response – the response, the thing that opens, that breaks – the response to this marvellous love of the Grace.

It is difficult without a strong will; and above all, above all the capacity to resist the temptation, which was the fatal temptation throughout all one's lives – because its power builds up. Each defeat gives it renewed force. But a tiny victory can dissolve it.

Oh, the most terrible of all is when one does not have the strength, the courage, something indomitable! How many times do they come to tell me, 'I want to die, I want to flee, I want to die.' I say, 'But die, then, die to yourself! No one is asking you to let your ego survive! Die to yourself since you want to.

Mother's Agenda, November 22nd, 1958

What is death?

A formidable campaign: On the 9th of December of this year (1958), Mother will leave.

It all began with some extremely violent attacks. So if your dream is not premonitory, then it must be the result of 'their' formation, by which they intend to disseminate the conviction everywhere, as much as possible, that this is the end.... Two years ago, when I had to retire to my room, a formidable campaign was set into operation upon all the Ashram people; and all those who were a little receptive, either in dreams or through an openness to suggestions, heard it clearly announced: 'On the 9th of December of this year *(1958),* Mother will leave. There's no doubt about it, it's sure.' It was said to me as well: 'This will be the end, you will leave.' It was repeated to everybody, everybody, a great many people heard it - they were virtually awaiting it. And this is why (you know how extremely ill I was at the time, I was really ill), this is why I didn't react, but all the same I didn't go to the lake *(the lake estate where Mother was to have gone on the 9th of December),* because I told myself, 'If anything happens there, it will be awkward - I had better not go.' But still I knew it wasn't true, I knew it.

Mother's Agenda, 11.2.61

Why make a drama out of death

I have had this experience, and I remember it even went on for several days; I saw all material circumstances as an absolute – an absolute that we perceive as an unfolding, but which is an eternally existing absolute. I had this experience, and at the same time I had a very clear perception of what falsehood is – the lie; what, from the psychological, the mental point of view, Sri Aurobindo, translating from the Sanskrit, called crookedness. We attribute the course of circumstances

1967, Terrace Darshan, Pondicherry, India

to our psychological reactions - and indeed, they are used momentarily because everything collaborates either consciously or unconsciously to make things be what they have to be - but things could be what they have to be without the intervention of this falsehood. I lived in that consciousness for several days, and it became apparent that this was what separated falsehood from truth. In this state of knowledge-consciousness, the distinction can be made between falsehood and truth; and when seen in that truth-consciousness, material circumstances change character.

Now I no longer have the experience of that state except as a memory, so I can't formulate it accurately. But what was very clear and comes very often - very often - is the perception of a superimposition of falsehood over a real fact. This brings us back to what I was telling you some time ago *(Agenda I of December 31st, 1960),* that everything is very simple in its truth, that human consciousness is what complicates everything. But the former was an even more total experience of it.

It is very interesting from the standpoint of death. I saw it once so clearly when someone (I no longer remember whom) had left his body. The word 'death' and all these human reactions seemed so foolish! So senseless, ignorant, stupid - false, without reality. There was simply something that shifted, like this (*Mother draws a curve showing a shift of consciousness from one mode of being to another*), and then we, in our false consciousness, made a drama out of it. But it was simply something evolving (*same gesture*).

Let me tell you about a recent occurrence. E. had sent a telegram saying that she had a perforated intestine (but it must have been something else because they operated on her only after several days, and when you are not operated on immediately in such cases, you die). Anyway, it was very serious and she was on the threshold of death – that much is certain. She wrote me a letter the day before the operation (what is interesting is that now she doesn't even remember what she wrote). It was a magnificent letter saying that she was conscious of the Divine Presence and of the Divine

Plan. 'Tomorrow they will operate on me,' she said. 'And I am entirely aware that this operation has ALREADY been done, that it is a fact accomplished by the Divine Will; otherwise it could be a fatal ordeal.' And she said she was conscious of the supreme Will's action, in a perfect peace. It was a magnificent letter. And the whole thing went off almost miraculously; she recovered in such a miraculous way that the surgeon himself said, I must congratulate you, to which she replied, 'How surprising! You did the operation!' 'Yes,' he said, 'we did the operation, but it is your body that willed to be healed, and I congratulate you for your body's willpower.' Of course she wrote to me that she knew who had been there to see that all went well. And this feeling of the thing being already accomplished is a beginning of the consciousness Sri Aurobindo speaks of in the 'Yoga of Self-Perfection', where one is simultaneously both here and there. Because, as Sri Aurobindo says, some people have managed to be entirely 'there', but what he has called the 'realization' is to be both there and here simultaneously.

Mother's Agenda, 18.4.61

I know all the people here. I know everything that's going on. I see it night and day.

I know all the people here. I know everything that's going on, I see it night and day. But I haven't seen this. Yes, there are ill-intentioned people, but they are even obliged to tell me so! There are people who ... oh, they almost wish I would leave, because they feel my presence as a constraint! They tell me so very frankly: 'As long as you're here, we're obliged to do the yoga, but we don't want to do the yoga, we want to live quietly; so if you weren't here, well, we wouldn't have to think about yoga anymore!' But they are a bunch of fools with no power in them at all. As I said, they are even forced to tell me their true feelings.

There are many - many - who think I am going to die and are making preparations so as not to be left completely out on the street when I go. I am aware of all this. But it's childishness - if I leave, they are right; if I don't, it doesn't matter!

Mother's Agenda, 22.4.61

Spiritual vibrations are quite clearly contagious.

Yes, of course – Sri Aurobindo told me so. But I stay behind, invisible! You don't even need to tell me things – you may tell me if you like, but it isn't necessary.

Now and then, I feel like saying outrageous things.... I almost said, 'How well I understand Sri Aurobindo - who passed to the other side!'

I have no intention of doing so, none at all. Not that I'm the least bit interested in all this outer jumble, not for that, but ... I promised Sri Aurobindo I would try.... So....

So, that's that.

Silence

Ah, but that's far more difficult than talking – far more! Far more, infinitely more difficult than talking. If you are a bit clear, transparent – it's enough just to be like this, at a given moment (*gesture of opening upwards*), to catch the Light, and then you can talk about it. Once you have seen it, you don't forget it. But to do....

This paucity, this narrowness.... It's relatively easy to get out of mental paucity, mental narrowness: one has only to pierce a hole, go beyond, and view things from above; and yes, immediately, it all widens. That's relatively easy. But this vital and PHYSICAL paucity, material narrowness ... ohh!

For mental narrowness, we know the means – one has only to go beyond it – we know the means. But this (Mother touches her body), however much one keeps bringing in, bringing in, bringing in the Light and the Force.... Yes, for a few moments

101

one can live a universal life, even in the sensations – but in the body....

For obviously it has to be done in this life. The body's progress can't be preserved, can it?

Of course not - that's just it!

It could be, yes, but to no avail. If all these cells which have become so conscious have to break up.... It would result in cells that are conscious, but mixed with.... What would it amount to, mixed with the sum total of all the unconscious cells of the earth? It would be useless.

Yes, it would be useless; I mean, perhaps after millions of years it would gradually snowball and have some effect - but that's just how Nature functions when left to her own interminable way - it is not yoga.

But once you have effected the transformation in your own body, will it be transmittable to others? Will your experience and your realization be transmittable?

It's a question of contagion. Spiritual vibrations are quite clearly contagious. Mental vibrations are contagious, and to a certain extent even vital vibrations are contagious (not often in their finer effects, but anyway, it's clear - a man's anger, for instance, spreads very easily). Well then, the quality of cellular vibrations should also be contagious.

Mother's Agenda, 25.4.61

This is what is promised. Now the Work must be done.

Some months ago, when this body had once again become a battlefield and was confronting all the obstacles, when it was suspended, asking itself whether ... it wasn't wondering intellectually, but asking for a kind of perception, wanting to touch something: it wondered which direction it was taking, which way things were going to tilt. And suddenly, in all the cells, there was this feeling (and I know where it came from): 'If we are dissolved out of this amalgam, if this assemblage is dissolved and can no longer go on, then we shall all go straight, straight as an arrow' - and it was like a marvellous flame - 'straight to rejoin Sri Aurobindo in his Supramental world, which is right here at our door.' And there was such joy! Such enthusiasm, such joy flooded all the cells! They didn't care at all whether or not they would be dissociated.... 'Oh,' they felt, 'so what!'

This was truly a decisive stage in the work of illuminating the body.

All the cells felt far more powerful than that stupid force trying to dissolve them; what is called 'death, left them entirely indifferent: 'What do we care? We shall go THERE and consciously participate in Sri Aurobindo's work, in the transformation of the world, one way or the other - here, there, like this, like that - what does it matter!'

This came more than a year ago, I think. It has never left. Never. All anxiety and all conscious tension have gone.

Only – there is an 'only' in all this – if there were a more liberal proportion between the 'refreshing' (if I may say so) freedom of solitude and the necessity for collective work, there would probably be fewer difficulties.... Towards the end of the first year after I retired upstairs (perhaps even before, but anyway, some time after I began doing japa while walking), I recall having such sessions up there! ... Had there been a personal goal, this goal was clearly attained; it is indescribable, absolutely beyond all imaginable or expressible splendour.

And that was when I received the Command from the Supreme, who was right here, this close (Mother presses her face). He told me, 'This is what is promised. Now the Work must be done.'

And not individual but collective work was meant. So naturally, because of the way it came, it was joyously accepted and immediately implemented.

But when I remember that experience and consider what I have now....

Well, what Sri Aurobindo did by leaving his body is somewhat equivalent, although far more total and complete and absolute – because he had that experience, he had that, he had it; I saw him, I saw him Supramental on his bed, sitting on his bed.

He has written: I am not doing it individually, for myself, but for the whole earth. And it was exactly the same thing for me – but oh, that experience! Nothing counted for me anymore: people, the earth – even the earth itself had absolutely no importance.

The clock strikes

Later, just before leaving:

But you know, this present state gives me the feeling that actually we know nothing at all, at all, at all – nothing at all. Everything else, everything leading to the spiritual life, to liberation and so forth – well, yes, it's all very well, all very well. But compared to what one must know to do this work....

Perhaps it's better not to know.

Because evidently I can't say that my experiences are the result of a mental aspiration or will or knowledge – I don't know, I don't know at all. I don't know how it should be, nor what it should be, nor anything at all. I don't know what should be done, I don't know what should not be done – nothing. It's truly a blind march (*gesture of groping along*), in a desert riddled with all possible traps and difficulties and obstacles – all this heaped together. Eyes blindfolded, knowing nothing (*same gesture of groping blindly*), one plods on.

The only thing to do is to be.

Mother's Agenda, 15.7.61

Aren't the places you go to in sleep the same as the ones you go to in death?

No, no, no. Most of the time in sleep, with very few exceptions, one is in contact with all that rises up from the subconscient: a cerebral subconscient, an emotive subconscient, a material subconscient; this is what produces ninety-nine percent of the dreams people have. Sometimes – usually – the mind goes wandering, but ninety-nine and a half percent of the time one remembers nothing when it returns, because the link is not properly established.

The purpose of sleep is to re-establish contact with the consciousness of *Sachchidananda*. But I don't think one person in a hundred does so! They enter into unconsciousness far more than into *Sachchidananda*.

Yet no two sleeps are the same, mon petit! And it's the same with deaths, no two are the same. But sleep and death are different because ... they are different STATES. As long as you have a body, you are not in the same state as when you are 'dead'. There is a period of seven days after the doctors declare you 'dead' when you are still in an intermediary state; but the actual state of death itself is completely different BECAUSE there is no longer this physical base.

Once when I was at Tlemcen with Théon (this happened twice, but I'm not sure about the second time because I was alone), my body was in a cataleptic state and I was in conscious trance.... It was a peculiar kind of catalepsy in the sense that my body could speak, though very slowly – Théon had taught me how to do it. But this is because the 'life of the form' always remains (this is what takes seven days to leave the body) and it

105

can even be trained to make the body move – the being is no longer there, but the life of the form can make the body move (in any case, utter words). However, this state is not without danger, the proof being that while I was working in trance, for some reason or other (which I no longer remember, but obviously due to some negligence on the part of Théon who was there to watch over me), the cord – I don't know what to call it – went snap! The link was cut, malevolently, and when it was time and I wanted to return, I could no longer re-enter my body. But I was still able to warn him: 'The cord is cut.' Then he used his power and knowledge to help me come back – but it was no joke! It was very difficult. And this is when I had the experience of the two different states, because the part that had gone out was now without the body's support – the link was cut. Then I knew. Of course, I was in a special state; I was doing a fully conscious work with all the vital power, and I was in control not only of my surroundings but.... You see, what happens is a kind of reversal of consciousness: you begin to belong to another world; you feel this quite distinctly. Théon instantly told me to concentrate (I was finding it all interesting – Mother laughs – I was making experiments and getting ready to go wandering off, but he was terribly scared that I would die on him!). He begged me to concentrate, so I concentrated on my body. When I re-entered, it hurt terribly, terribly – an excruciating pain, like plunging into a hell.

Into a...?

Into a hell *(Mother laughs)*.
  It was frightful. It doesn't last long.
  He made me drink half a glass of cognac (he always made me take some every day after the trance because I would work in trance for more than an hour, which is generally a forbidden practice). Still, I am quite sure that with anybody but me and him, this would have been the end. I would not have re-entered.
  So I know a little bit, even in my outermost consciousness. A little bit, that's all.

No, sleep is something else. Yes, something else. It's more like a relapse into Inconscience – a sort of invasion of tamas.

Mother's Agenda, 5.8.1961

Last time you said, "They are burned, or shut up in a box without air and light - fully conscious...."

And it is hideously true.

But what should be done then? Should people wait, or what?

I have looked at this a great deal, but ... socially, conventionally, it's impossible - there's nothing else to do. The living take their stand with the living, naturally. So the only thing I've seen is that, as always, there must be a grace associated with that state, and probably people see ONLY what they are able to see without being upset.

I know this because when the body became like that - it was more than three-quarters dead (*last April*) - and people were taking care of me, doing everything for me, I was fully conscious, FULLY, but I couldn't.... I was like a dead person. And it wasn't that I couldn't move, but I couldn't manifest anything - I didn't want to! I was in a state of total bliss, and couldn't have cared less about what was going to happen. Well, that's what I think must happen to those who ... who die in a state of grace - it's true, some people die well and others don't. It all depends on one's state of consciousness.

If at death you withdraw from physical circumstances, from ordinary physical consciousness, and unite with the great universal Force, or the divine Presence, then all these little things.... It's not that you're not conscious of them - you are very conscious: conscious of what others are doing, conscious of everything, but ... it's not important.

But for those who are attached to people and things when they die, it must be a hellish torment.

Hellish.

107

But then, is it better to be buried or burned?

Had you asked me this question a week ago, I would unhesitatingly have said "buried" - and advised people not to do it too quickly, to wait for external signs of decomposition.

Now, because of this, I can't say any more. I just can't say.

I have the feeling I am learning a lot of things about this transition called death. It's starting to become thinner and thinner, more and more unreal. It is very interesting.

Silence

One may be in a state of consciousness where the body is nothing but a burden – it's unresponsive, or it's too deteriorated and there's nothing more to be done with it, or one hasn't been created to try to make it immortal (which, after all, is something very exceptional). Within the great mass of humanity, many bodies are no longer good for anything, and in such cases it may very well be a relief to be separated from your body abruptly, instead of waiting for a slow decomposition. So... once again I am saying to myself, "A rash and hasty judgment – the judgment of Ignorance."

I can't say. Each individual has to FEEL it and, if he's conscious enough, say what he would like.

But each time I ask my body what IT would like, all the cells say, "No, no! We are immortal, we want to be immortal. We're not tired, we're ready to struggle for centuries if necessary; we have been created for immortality and we want immortality."

It is very interesting.

Very interesting. And Pavitra was telling me recently that the causes of aging and decay are now being very seriously and deeply investigated. Some quite interesting discoveries are being made: that the cell is immortal, and that aging results merely from a combination of circumstances. This research is tending towards the conclusion that aging is merely a bad habit - which seems to be true. Which means that when you LIVE in

108

the Truth-Consciousness, Matter is not in contradiction to that Consciousness.

And this is just what I am realizing (I don't think it's anything unique or exceptional): the closer one draws to the cell itself, the more the cell says, "But I am immortal!" Only it must become conscious. But this takes place almost automatically: the brain cells are very conscious; the cells of the hands and arms of musicians are very conscious; with athletes and gymnasts, the cells of the entire body are wonderfully conscious. So, being conscious, those cells become conscious of their principle of immortality and say, "Why would I want to grow old? Why!" They don't want to grow old. It is very interesting.

So all the ideas I used to have about death, all the things I have said about death, practically all the things I have consciously DONE *(for people who died)* - oh! I have realized that all this, too, belongs to the past, and to a past of Ignorance. Here also, I will probably have other things to say later.

If I ever say them.

As soon as you speak, most of the knowledge escapes. It becomes what Sri Aurobindo calls a "representation", an image - it is not THE thing.

Mother's Agenda, 16.10.62

I have always observed very carefully every time somebody died here in the Ashram...

I have always observed very carefully every time somebody died here in the Ashram, and well (one or two persons have died since that experience, in particular the old doctor's sister), well, since then it has been ABSOLUTELY DIFFERENT. It was something I saw from above. There was no longer any mystery. But if you ask me to explain... That I can't – words, the mind, no. But the POSITION of the consciousness was different – the position of the consciousness. Altogether different.

And IN THE PRESENT CASE, the conscious power would mean the power to give or prevent death equally; to effect the

109

necessary movement of forces – almost ... almost an action on the cells, a mechanical action on the cells. With that power, you can give death, you can prevent death.

But there is NO LONGER any of that sensation people have of a brutal clash between life and its opposite, death - death is not the opposite of life! At that moment I understood, and I never forgot: death is NOT the opposite of life, it is not the opposite of life. It's a sort of change in the cells' functioning or in their organization....

When I say all this now, I try to pull back a deep-buried memory. But that's the point. Once you have understood that (all that you understand, you can do), once you've understood that, you can do it. Then it's very simple: you can easily stop the thing from going this way or that way; you can go like that or like this or like that (*Mother seems to handle forces or shift the position of the consciousness*). Then it almost becomes child's play to make someone die or make someone live! But that is better left unsaid.

But it will surely come! In how many years, I don't know, but the thing has become plain. And to me (as I said the other day), to me it seemed quite a central secret - not the most central of all, no, but fairly central with regard to life on earth.

It's ... of course, it would mean a new phase for life on earth.

Mother's Agenda, 16.3.63

Well, death is a waste and that's that.

But after death, it's finished.

It's finished.

It's finished, for sure!

Consequently, it's a waste. We are consoled by being told, "No, death isn't a waste, because everything goes into the general work" - it's not true! It's not true, it's a pure waste.

It's true on the mental or vital level, but on the physical level it's not true.

On the physical level, it's a pure waste. The mind and vital are another affair, that's not interesting: we have known for a very long time that their life doesn't depend on the body - it depends on the body only in order to manifest. That's another affair. I am speaking of the body, that's what interests me: the body's cells. Well, death is a waste and that's that.

Well, yes! But there's no point in consoling oneself by saying "Next life", the next life everything must be done all over again.

Everything must be done all over again, all over again. That's terrible!

There's no doubt, the Transformer must carry out the transformation in his lifetime.

So I don't mean to be pessimistic, but if it ends in a death, I will have wasted all my work.

Not for the consciousness, naturally - all that is conscious remains conscious, eternally conscious - but for the cells of the body, the work has to be done all over again.

Mother's Agenda, 26.8.64

I wanted to leave my body...

But when you want to be absolutely sincere and not to kid yourself, in other words, not to be satisfied with explanations of appearances, you realize that you know nothing. All the

111

experiences I have with people leaving their bodies, the more I have, the more ... *puzzling* it is. For instance, not very long ago, I had an experience with L. The night before she officially died, she came to me in an absolutely concrete manner: she had settled down and didn't want to leave me - wherever I went she followed me. She seemed to be clinging to me, talking to me, asking me questions - officially she was still alive. And there was a sort of tall being (those beings are connected to Death; I don't know their exact name, in the traditions they have been given all kinds of names - those are things I don't know at all theoretically). This time, a being of that sort was there, and it was as if he had given her permission to be there for a certain time, as if he were in charge of her and of taking her away once the time was up (all this without words, but "understood"). Then she told me (after literally "sticking" to me: I couldn't do anything anymore, she was taking up all my time), she told me, "I wanted to leave my body on..." (I don't remember exactly, it was a Darshan day, November 24th or August 15th, but if it was August 15th, then she came to see me on the 14th). So I answered her, "Listen, today isn't the 15th yet; if you want to leave on the 15th, you should go back now." (That was to get rid of her! It was so concrete, you know, like when you have someone in your room and can't get rid of him.) Finally, I looked at that tall individual who was standing there perfectly peacefully and as if indifferent (he was there as an active permission), and I ... I didn't tell him, but "communicated" to him that perhaps it was time to take her away. And prrt! she left instantly - he was awaiting my order. None of this corresponds to any active knowledge on my part: that's just how it happened. And when she came back into her body in the morning, she told those waiting around her, "I spent the night with Mother, I was with her, I didn't leave her. She sent me back, but now I am going back to her." I was told this in the morning. A few hours later, she died. So the agreement is excellent, everything tallies. But her intention was not to leave me after her death (she came in the night with the idea that she was dead and that she was leaving me). Well, after she really died, I didn't get a SINGLE sign of her! ...

So I sat there wondering, "Is there really a difference of consciousness between the time when there is life in the body and the time when one leaves?..." It was a problem for me for days.

Things of this sort, you understand!

And the more I go into the details, the more I ... The more you feel YOU-KNOW-NOTHING. What people call "knowing" is wanting to define, regulate and organize things - that doesn't correspond to ANYTHING.

Mother's Agenda, 26.8.64

Could what is called "death" be by chance a multitude of different things?

For so many, so many years I have had all kinds of experiences. For about sixty years I have been constantly looking after people who are said to be "dying" - constantly. Well, there are almost as many cases as there are people - there are categories, but the cases are innumerable (and I am not referring to external cases, to the material event: I am referring to the inner cases). This is to say that I have been put in almost constant contact with the phenomenon, and yet, it remains a problem.... At least twice in this existence, I have gone through what people call "death" - and both times the experience was different. The experience was different, yet the apparent fact was the same.

And if I look at it in a certain way (explanations, of course, are meaningless), if I look at it in a certain way, I mean, to have the true key ... one has it only with the Power. Well, that Power...

Mother shakes her head

It's hard to explain if I want to make myself understood. For instance, many times (many times, very often), people told me

113

they wanted to die for some reason or other; and by doing a certain thing, it happened. The "thing" wasn't always the same, but the result was in appearance always the same: the person left his or her body. I even had near me, at least twice, very clearly and precisely, people who were supposedly "dead", who had left their body in that way, and they knew nothing about it! Therefore, for that part of their being, it made no difference. And it has also happened that I've "resurrected", as it is called, someone who had been declared dead. This is to tell you that all the various possibilities (not all, but many), all that has been shown to me.

Naturally, it is always a movement of the consciousness (that brings about death) and a certain movement of the will, but...

What I was wondering about today (not "wondering" – words are always wrong – because it isn't mental, I wasn't wondering mentally), but suddenly there came in front of me, like this (*gesture indicating a cinema screen*): could what is called "death" be by chance a multitude of different things?... We say "life", "death", and we oppose that death to life – could it be, by chance, that what people call "death" is a multitude of different things, of different possibilities?

Silence

What is it?

Human science answers: there is an analogous phenomenon in all cases – decomposition. But that... We are in a constant state of decomposition – everything, all life is constantly in a state of decomposition and transformation; all the food we absorb is constantly in a state of decomposition. So...

It may simply be the incompleteness, I mean the limitation of our vision, our perception: we see the details too much instead of seeing the whole. You know, I had a sudden feeling with the tension of the concentration: What is the physical perception of the totality of the physical world? What is the consciousness of the totality of the physical world? Isn't, for that consciousness, isn't all that we call death and life a phenomenon analogous to the phenomenon of decomposition, assimilation, transformation that takes place in every living being?

It's enough to leave you completely dazed!

It is the cellular transformation, the progressive cellular transformation which is, on the scale of the human being (of the human being, of the animal, etc), what we call "death".

We will talk about it again.

Mother's Agenda, 28.4.65

The vast majority of human beings have a collective destiny.

I've received a certain number of questions from the older pupils (not the young children, the older pupils) on "death", the conditions of death, why there are so many accidents at present, and so on. I have already answered two pupils. Of course, the answer is on a mental level, but with an attempt to go beyond.

There is that sort of mental logic which wants... yes, which wants things to be deduced from one another according to that logic, and so they have reached... impossible questions.

(the text of the questions:)

Are the time and manner of death always chosen by the soul? In large human destructions through bombings, floods, earthquakes, have all the souls chosen to die together at that time?

The vast majority of human beings have a collective destiny. For them the question does not arise. One who has an individualized psychic being can survive even in the midst of collective catastrophes, if such is the choice of his soul.

*How is the soul conscious of being and existing after death,
once it is separated from its physical vital and mental beings?*

The soul is a spark of the Supreme Divine, I do not see how the
Lord needs a body in order to be conscious of being.

It's nothing very new, but it's a broadening of the
consciousness. And all these questions have in fact been coming
into the atmosphere lately, giving at first the impression that
man knows nothing about death – he doesn't know what it is,
doesn't know what happens, he has built all kinds of hypotheses
but has no certainties. And by pressing on – by insisting and
pressing on – I have reached the conclusion... that there is
really no such thing as death.

There is only an appearance, and an appearance based on a
limited outlook. But there is no radical change in the vibration
of consciousness. This came as an answer to a sort of anguish
– there was in the cells a sort of anguish at not knowing what
death really is; a sort of anguish, like that. And the response
was very clear and persistent: it was that the consciousness
alone can know, because... because the importance attached to
the difference of state is a merely superficial difference based
on an ignorance of the phenomenon in itself. One who could
retain a means of communication would be able to say that as
far as he himself is concerned, it doesn't make much difference.

But this is something being worked out at the moment. There
still remain grey areas and some details of experience are
missing. So it would be better to wait, it seems to me, until the
knowledge is more complete, because rather than give an
approximation with assumptions, it would be better to tell the
complete fact with the total experience. So we'll put it off till
later.

*But you say there is no difference – when one is on the other
side, does one go on having or is one able to have the perception
of the physical world?*

Yes, yes, it is so.

The perception of beings, of... (Satprem meant seagulls over the sea, trees, the pretty sunshine on the earth).

Yes, exactly.

Only, instead of having a perception... You leave a sort of illusory state and a perception which is one of appearances, but you do have a perception. That is, at certain times I had the perception, I was able to see the difference, but of course, the experience wasn't total (it wasn't total in the sense that it was cut short by people), so it's better to wait awhile before we talk about it.

But the perception is there.

Not absolutely identical, but with an effectiveness which is sometimes greater in itself. But it's not really perceived by the other side. I don't know how to explain. I've had the example (not an example: it was lived with the full perception) of a being who lived with me for years, who remained in perfectly conscious contact after he had left his body (and left it quite materially), and who didn't merge but closely associated himself with another living being and in this association went on living the life of his OWN CONSCIOUSNESS. I can give neither the names nor the facts about all this, but it's as concrete as can be. And it's going on. All this has been seen – I've been seeing it for a long time, but just this morning it came back as an illustration of the new knowledge. Extraordinarily concrete (the "association") in its effects, changing the capacities and movements of the other's consciousness. And consciously – an absolutely conscious life. And it's the same consciousness that was conscious during the phase when there was no body left at all and the presence was visible only in the night vision.

There are other cases.

This one is very close and intimate, which is why I have been able to follow it in all its details.

But it's clear, precise and EVIDENT only with this new vision, because (how can I explain?...) I knew this – I knew it before, I was aware of it – but I saw it again with the new consciousness, the new way of seeing, and then the understanding was total, the perception was total, absolutely concrete, with elements that were completely missing – convincing elements that were completely missing in the first perception, which was a vital-mental knowledge. While this is a knowledge of the consciousness of the cells.

But all this would only be interesting with all the facts (which I can't give). So I'd like to have a more complete and "impersonal" experience, I might say, I mean not illustrated by facts but an overall vision of the process. Then I will be able to talk about it. It will come.

Mother's Agenda, 7.3.67

It was as if the body were asking, "What attitude" (that's what provided the link), "What attitude should I have? What should I do?..." Because there was the vision of life, death, of all circumstances, everything was there. The full knowledge of everything. Oh, the whole part about death was very, very interesting, and how mankind has tried to understand, how there have been all kinds of solutions (that is, partial attitudes), and all of it was part of the Whole.

So the conclusion ... Oh, at that time I could have said many things about all the different intellectual and even spiritual attitudes of mankind.... There aren't big differences. The spiritual (what's commonly called "spiritual") boils down to the whole attempt at finding the Divine again by annulling the creation - that's what has been regarded as spiritual life (that's why the word got distorted). To annul the creation in order to find the Divine again... And then, NOW: the vision of now. We are obviously drawing nearer to the moment of possibility - that is clear. It's a question of time - of course, it can't be on the human scale, but we are on the borderline.

You understand, behind this whole earth evolution, there is, with a greater or lesser degree of consciousness (it's an unexpressed need rather than a precise consciousness), the need to live the Divine - or to put it differently, the need to live divinely. And it is clear that what was translated

118

into different religions was solutions found individually ("found", and perhaps partially lived); and here (*in India*), there was this solution: in order to really become the Divine again, the creation should be done away with. That is, the Nirvanic solution. And instinctively - instinctively - mankind felt death to be the negation of the Divine. But like every negation, it had the capacity to lead and open the way. The solution of Christianity wasn't quite new, it was the adaptation of an ancient solution: a life in other worlds - which was translated into that quite childish conception of heaven. But that was a conception for public use: a life in the presence of the Divine, exclusively taken up with the Divine, and so you would sing and ... Touchingly simple.

Anyway, they conceived of a world (not a material one) in which a divine life had been realized. In the ancient Indian traditions, there had also been a first hint of divine worlds, as a sort of reaction to that Nirvanism - if we want to be divine, we must stop being, or if the Divine wants to be pure, he must stop manifesting! ... So all that was like clumsy attempts to find the means, and perhaps at the same time like inner preparations, to make people capable of really making contact with the Divine. Then there was that great reaction of the cult of Matter, which has been VERY useful to knead it and make it less unconscious of itself: it has forcibly brought consciousness back into Matter. So perhaps all that has been a sufficient preparation for the moment of the Total Manifestation to have come (*gesture of descent*).

Mother's Agenda, 19.8.67

Death is the phenomenon of decentralization...

"Death is the phenomenon of decentralization and scattering of the cells making up the physical body.

"Consciousness is, in its very nature, immortal, and in order to manifest in the physical world, it clothes itself

119

in material forms that are durable to a greater or lesser degree.

"The material substance is in process of transformation to become an increasingly perfect and durable multiform mode of expression for that consciousness."

Mother's Agenda, 18.5.68

"How can one say with certainty that the physical body is dead?"

Only when it decomposes.

Mother's Agenda, 28.9.68

I only call Mother and Her Grace and as soon as I do it everything becomes all right and quite normal.

There's something that's not at all part of my role here near you, but I think it's urgent and I should tell you about it. It's about G.

Ah!

Yes, he is struggling with death. He came to see me and explained everything. For two years he's been fighting against heart attacks. He has never told anyone about it, he has immense trust in the Grace. He told me, "I've had wonderful experiences in which I called Mother, Mother came, and in a moment the danger was repulsed." (That recurred several times.) He told me, for instance, that he read the February Bulletin a hundred times over and found in it an immense help, precisely where you speak of the descending Presence that makes everything disappear as if it were unreal. But anyway, he has reached a point where his body has become very weak. So he's written a letter to you:

(extracts from the letter in English)

"Since about two years my health is not normal. Not only in abnormal condition but it is so serious that struggle is going between life and death. It began with a little pain in the chest and an uneasiness in the heart. After some time it slowly affected the whole body, so much that many a time I feel as if it will collapse just now. At such moments I only call Mother and Her Grace, and as soon as I do it everything becomes all right and quite normal.

I never consulted any doctor or tried any treatment. Even I did not let the people around me ever know about it, as I believe, from my childhood, that such attacks should not be brought in words .... Sometimes, things happened very inexplicably, as more than two times I felt some force entering in my body to bring its end at once. But as I was always ready to face it with the call for the Grace every time it was forced to leave me enveloping with Grace. One night (mostly attacks come at night) I saw a woman aged forty or forty-five with dreadful face declaring, 'I am Death and have come to take you. Now you cannot escape.' But I do not know how it happened that I got up and sat in my bed, challenging her with the Call of Mother and Her Grace. On this, the woman laughed, making her face at me, and to my surprise I heard her laugh with my physical ears and saw her with my physical eyes. But Mother, she disappeared in no time as soon as Grace's presence was there, and I found myself again in full strength, surrounded with Grace and Grace only. In this struggle I also have the experience of my real 'I' in the heart of the Mother with infinite strength. I found Mother's Presence - no, Mother Herself - hours and hours with me (behind or in front). Also I saw Mother in Her quite young body, so much different that for a moment I could not recognize Mother but Mother took me in Her Lap with immense Love....

After a long silence

This woman, did he see her with open or closed eyes?

With wide open eyes.

Then it's in the subtle physical. Did she look like someone he knows?

I don't know.

(Mother goes into a long contemplation)

I'll see .... We'll try .... In a few days, ask him to come and see you to tell you how he feels.

Mother's Agenda, 17.9.69

It's only when the power of concentration disappears that the cells scatter.

I've had a revelation.

Ah!

It was very interesting. That is, I was completely silent, and all of a sudden, it came, and as always it kept insisting until I noted it down.

It came in the wake of a question: "What is death?..." But then, the answer wasn't at all on the ordinary plane, which means that the mind was perfectly silent.

It came like this, imperative *(Mother laughs):*

Death is the decentralization of the consciousness contained in the body's cells.

With a whole world of perceptions at the same time *(Mother makes a gesture around her),* like a general terrestrial consciousness, with examples showing that it's only when the consciousness contained in the cells is decentralized that one is dead. Otherwise, nothing, not even the heart stopping, can cause death.

Naturally, this decentralization stems from innumerable

causes, but they are causes we might call psychological. And the cells contained in the body, or composing the body, are held in form by a centralization of the consciousness in them, and as long as that power of concentration is there, the body cannot die. It's only when the power of concentration disappears that the cells scatter. And then one dies. Then the body dies.

The sequel was like this....

Mother takes another note

The habitual concentration of Nature (produced by Nature) is a MECHANICAL concentration which is subject to all sorts of mechanical laws too, but ... *(Mother reads out her note)* Here is what came:

The very first step towards immortality is to replace the mechanical centralization by a willed centralization.

... which comes from the inner Presence, which means that through its will, the divine Presence concentrates the cells.

There.

In English, I put it like this:

Death is the consequence of the decentralisation of the Consciousness contained in the cells composing the body.

And then:

This centralisation produced by Nature is mechanical and it must be replaced by a willed centralisation.

Mother's Agenda, 17.12.69

It's good that men don't know that death doesn't exist – otherwise many would go!

Because, of course, the first stage once one knows that... if one knew that death really isn't such a total difference as people think, if they knew what it really is without having the inner realization of self-giving, all those who felt hurt would say, "I'm going!..."

All at once I understood that, and I said to myself it's an infinite Wisdom again, an infinite Grace that man does not know – does not know what death is, he thinks it's the end.

Mother's Agenda, 7.2.70

But why do we die? Why do we live to die? – That's idiotic!"

I remember the first time (that was very long ago, more than sixty years ago), the first time I asked, "But why do we die? Why do we live to die? – That's idiotic!" Then I was made to understand that all that we see as 'forms' is...*(gesture in perpetual movement)*. It's our clenched little consciousness, a clenched consciousness which makes it all appear a 'momentous' phenomenon: we are small, we grow big, and in the end we dissolve. But everything is like that! There are very few things – very few – that are eternal. They have a different quality. It's the first experience you get when you contact that which is eternal: it has a different vibratory quality... And then, that will to make this last (*Mother points to her body*), this which is made, entirely made of wrong movements – wrong movements and constantly in movement, constantly changing, constantly (*same gesture*).... As Sri Aurobindo said, "You want to make your body and everything around it last as it is?" – No, thank you! (*Mother laughs*) To last is, in fact, to become conscious, fully conscious in the eternal world.

Mother's Agenda, 18.4.70

Fear of the dead

But why did you bury me alive?

It is clear that if this experience becomes natural, spontaneous and constant, death can no longer exist: even for this, I mean (*Mother touches her body*).

There's something I SENSE there, without being able to express or understand it mentally. There must be some difference, even in the behavior of the cells, when you leave your body.

It must be another phenomenon that takes place.

During all that period of concentration and meditation on what happens in a body after death (I am speaking of the body's experience after what is now called "death"), well, several times the same kind of vision came to me.... I had been told (shown and told) of certain saints whose bodies did not decompose (there's one here, there was one in Goa – fantastic stories). Naturally, people always romanticize those things, but there remains the material fact of a saint who died in Goa, left his body in Goa, but whose body didn't decompose. I don't know the story in all its details, but the body was removed from India, taken away to China and remained buried there, in Hong-Kong, I believe (or somewhere in that region) for a time; then it was taken out, brought back here, buried again. For ten or twelve years it stayed buried in those two places: it didn't decompose. It dried out, became mummified (dried out, that is, dehydrated), but it remained preserved. Well, this fact was presented to me several times as ONE of the possibilities.

Which means, to tell the truth, that everything is possible.

But what I was shown clearly and what I saw was ... (I have difficulty talking because it all came to me in English: Sri Aurobindo was there and it was in English), it was the stupidity and carelessness, really, the ignorance - the stupid ignorance and I-couldn't-care-less attitude the living have towards the dead. That's something frightful. Frightful... Frightful. I've heard stories from everywhere, all sorts of appalling things... For instance, one of the stories (it took place while Sri Aurobindo was here): there was a disciple whose son died (or at least they thought him dead), and as they weren't Hindus, they didn't burn him: they buried him. Then at night, his son came to him and told him ... you see, he saw his son at the window, knocking at the window and telling him, "But why did you bury me alive?" (I don't know in what language, but anyway...) And that idiot of a father thought, "I'm dreaming"!! Then the next day, long afterwards, he had second thoughts and asked himself, "What if we take a look?" And they found him turned over in his coffin.

When the man told me the story and how he found it quite natural to think, "I am dreaming," I can't find words to tell my indignation at that moment, when I saw that ... you know, it's such a crass, such an inert stupidity! It didn't even occur to him how he would have felt if the thing had happened to HIM. It didn't even occur to him!

There was another case of a man who had been brought to the cremation ground, but a torrential rain started - no question of burning him. They left him there and said, "We'll burn him tomorrow." But the next morning when they came, he wasn't there any more! (*Laughing*) He was gone. But that's not all: thirty years later, he returned (he was a Raja): he had been picked up by sannyasins, taken into solitude, and had become a sannyasin, until, thirty years later, for God knows what reason, he thought it best to go and claim his possessions, so he returned with proofs that he was indeed the same man... (*It is the story of the Raja of Bhaowal, which created a sensation in the Indian press around 1930.*)

I have heard countless stories of that kind, which show the point to which men ... They want to get rid of the dead, don't they! And the faster the better.

I remember someone who told me (someone who claimed to be a sage), he told me, "But if it's untrue that the same beings reincarnate many times, then the dead increase more and more in number, and the atmosphere is going to be terribly crowded with all those dead! ... They'll become a plague. What will we do with all that? They will be far more numerous than the living and will crowd everything - what will we do with all that?" There, you see the type of reflection.

Silence

The attitude of the living towards the dead is one of the most loathsome expressions of mankind's selfish ignorance.

It's either a complete I-couldn't-care-less attitude, or else, "Ohh, anything to get rid of that!" I have some children here (they're no longer children), who live here with their fathers and mothers (who aren't very old), and some of those children told me "dreams" in which they saw their fathers or mothers dead and coming to them ... and they sent them back violently, saying, "You're dead, you've got no right to come and bother us"! ...

You're dead, you've got no right to come and bother us. There you are.

That's ... few will be frank enough to say so, but it's very widespread.

Many things must change before a little bit of truth can manifest - that's all I can say.

Mother's Agenda, 10.8.63

My first action is always the same: send the Peace...

I have received your note and it didn't surprise me, because just about a month ago I received what seemed like an SOS from your mother, telling me your father was rapidly declining. I have done what I could, mainly to bring in some tranquillity, some calm, some inner peace. But I haven't done.... You see, there are always two possibilities when people are so seriously ill: they can be helped to die quickly, or else made to linger on for a very long time. When I have no outer or inner indications,

127

all I ever do is apply the consciousness for the best to happen to them (the best from the soul's standpoint, of course).

Do you know whether your father has expressed any wish?

According to my mother's letter, he says he no longer particularly cares to live, that his days are so miserable....

But he still doesn't want to pass away? Is he suffering a great deal?

He's suffering.

(*Mother remains silent for a moment, then says:*) Over the years I have had a considerable number of experiences in this realm, and my first action is always the same: send the Peace (I do this in all cases, for everyone) and apply the Force, the Power of the Lord, for the best thing to happen. Some people are very sick, sick to the point where there is no hope, where they cannot be cured, where the end is coming; but they sense that their souls must still need to have certain experiences, so they hang on - they don't want to die. In such cases I apply the Force for them to last as long as possible. In other cases, on the contrary, they are weary of suffering, or indeed the soul has finished its experience and desires to be liberated. In such a case, if I am sure of it, sure that they themselves are expressing the desire to depart, it's over in a few hours – I say this with certainty because I've had a considerable number of experiences. There is a certain force which goes out and does what is necessary. I haven't done either of these things for your father – neither to prolong his life (because when people are suffering it's not very kind to prolong their lives indefinitely), nor to finish it, because I didn't know – one can't do either without knowing the person's conscious wish.

As for your mother, she must have been thinking of me, for otherwise she wouldn't have come in that way – she would have come through you (it's different when things come through you). But she came to me directly, so I thought that for some reason she must have remembered me. I don't know. And I looked and said to myself (it came just like that), 'Now that she will be left all alone, why doesn't she come here?' I haven't done anything about that, either, one way or the other.

That's odd – the same thought has been coming to me these last three or four days: why doesn't she come here?

It didn't come from me, you understand; it didn't stem from a construction made by me: it came from outside. 'Why doesn't she come here?' I wondered.

The same thought came to me three or four times.

Then she is thinking about it – perhaps not consciously, but in her subconscient. It happened some time ago. I even spoke to Sujata about it and said that someone over there was calling you. Did she tell you?

No.

That your mother was pulling on you?

She had Z write to me.

As I said, I have done nothing, neither one way nor the other. So don't do anything. You know, from time to time when people are very sick, something comes out of them to indicate their will. But one has to be present, one has to hear it.

Silence

There was an experience like that quite recently. A.'s mother was ill – old and seriously ill. Seeing her declining, A. wrote to me: 'If the time has come, make it happen quickly – don't let her suffer.' Then I saw very clearly that there was still

129

something in her which didn't want to go; and when I applied the Force for the best to happen she suddenly began to recover! It must have coincided with a kind of inner aspiration in her – no more fever, she was feeling well. And A. began preparing to come back here. 'If she's recovering,' he said, 'there's no longer any point in my staying!' The same evening she had a relapse and he sent me a telegram. Meanwhile (it was evening) I had gone upstairs to 'walk'; suddenly The Will came (which is a very, very rare thing), The Will: 'Enough, now it must finish – it's enough as it is.' Within half an hour she was dead.

These things are very interesting. They must form part of the work I have come on earth to do. Because even before encountering Théon, before knowing anything, I had experiences at night, certain types of activities looking after people who were leaving their bodies – and with a knowledge of the process; I didn't know what I was doing nor did I seek to know, yet I knew exactly what had to be done and I did it. I was around twenty.

As soon as I came upon Théon's teaching (even before meeting him personally), and read and understood all kinds of things which I hadn't known before, I began to work quite systematically. Every night, at the same hour, I was working to construct – between the purely terrestrial atmosphere and the psychic atmosphere – a path of protection across the vital, so that people wouldn't have to pass through it (for those who are conscious but without knowledge it's a very difficult passage – infernal). I was preparing this path, doing this work (it must have been around 1903 or 1904, I don't remember exactly) for months and months and months. All sorts of extraordinary things happened during that time – extraordinary. I could tell long stories....

Then, when I went to Tlemcen, I told Madame Théon about it. 'Yes,' she told me, 'it is part of the work you have come on earth to do. Everyone with even a slightly awakened psychic being who can see your Light will go to your Light at the moment of dying, no matter where they die, and you will help them to pass through.' And this work is constant. Constant it has given me a considerable number of experiences concerning what happens to people when they leave their bodies. I've had all sorts of experiences, all kinds of examples – it's really very interesting.

Lately it has increased, become more precise.

There is a boy here, V., who is especially interested in what happens at the moment of death (this seems to be one reason why he has reincarnated). He's a conscious boy, a remarkable clairvoyant, and he has a power. And we have had (how to put it?) some quite interesting correlations of experiences concerning people who pass away here. Extremely interesting and extraordinarily precise: he sends word to me, I reply, and at night when the disincarnated person comes he says, 'Mother has done this and says to do that,' and the person does it. And we don't need to speak – such precision!

This happens in sleep?

He might do this work in sleep, or sometimes in meditation, or in a kind of trance he enters into – it depends on the case.

I will give you a concrete example, then you'll understand. When I.B. was killed, I had to gather up all his states of being and activities, which had been dispersed by the violence of the accident – it was terrible, he was in a dreadful state of dispersion. For two or two and a half days the doctors fought in the hope of reviving him, but it was impossible.

During those two days I gathered up all his consciousness, all of it; I collected it over his body, to the point where, when it had come and formed itself there, such vitality, such life was coming back into his body that after some hours the doctors believed he would be saved. But it couldn't last (it wasn't possible – a part of the brain had come out). Well, when not only his soul but his mental being, his vital being, and all the rest had been properly collected and organized over his body and had realized that the body had become quite unusable, it was over – they gave up the body and it was over.

I was keeping I.B. near me because I already had the idea of putting him immediately back into another body – his soul was not satisfied, it had not finished its experience (there was a whole combination of circumstances) and it wanted to continue to live on earth. Then, that night, his inner being went to find V., lamenting, saying he was dead and hadn't wanted to die, that he had lost his body and wanted to continue to live. V. was very perplexed. He let me know about it in the morning: 'Here's what has happened.' I sent word to him of what I was doing, that I was keeping I.B. in my atmosphere and that he should stay very calm and not get excited, for I was going to put him back into a body as soon as possible – I already had something in view. The same evening I.B. again went to find V., with the same complaint. V. told him very clearly, 'Here is what Mother says, here is what she is going to do; come now, be calm and don't torment yourself.' And he saw in I.B.'s face that he had understood (the inner being was taking on I.B.'s physical appearance, naturally); his face relaxed, he became content.

He went away and he never came back. That is, he stayed tranquilly with me, until I was able to put him into C'.s child.

This correlation in the work is very interesting because it has quite practical effects – V. was able to communicate exactly what I had to say to I.B., and I.B. understood better through him than through me directly (because I do the work, but don't have time to deal with all the details, to tell each individual what to do).

I was telling you the other day how vexing it is that we are all on different planes all the time, but on that particular plane it works very well with this boy – on this one point, this tiny, precise point concerning the moment of leaving the body. We can do interesting work this way.

Is one snatched up by the vital zone upon leaving the body?

No, it depends.

It depends entirely upon the way people die: on the way they leave their bodies, on what is around them, on the atmosphere created for them.

If they call me, then it goes well.

There have been very, very few cases, a quite minimal number, when people have called (not very sincerely) and their call hasn't had much effect. But even these people have a protection. There was a woman here, an old woman who was not very sincere (she didn't live here – she only came to visit) and the last time she visited she fell ill and died. Then I saw that she was completely dispersed into all her desires, all her memories, all her attachments ... and it had all been scattered here and there, into all sorts of things (one part of her was seeking, seeking where to go and what to do); anyway, it was rather pitiful. Afterwards I was asked, 'How did it happen? She was calling all the time.' I replied that I had not heard her call – it must not have been very sincere, only a formula.

But it's very rare that people get no response.

Not long ago M.'s sister died (psychologically, she was in a terrible state – she had no faith). Well, on that day, just when I came to know that she was passing away, I remember being upstairs in the bathroom communicating with Sri Aurobindo, having a sort of conversation with him (it happens very often), and I asked him, 'What happens to such people when they die here at the Ashram?' 'Look,' he replied, and I saw her passing away; and on her forehead, I saw Sri Aurobindo's symbol in a SOLID golden light (not very luminous, but very concrete). There it was. And with the presence of this sign the psychological state no longer mattered – nothing touched her. And she departed tranquilly, tranquilly. Then Sri Aurobindo told me, 'All who have lived at the Ashram and who die there have automatically the same protection, whatever their inner state.'

I can't say I was surprised, but I admired the mighty power by which the simple fact of having been here and died here was sufficient to help you to the utmost in that transition.

But there are all sorts of cases. Take N.D., for example, a man who lived his whole life with the idea of serving Sri Aurobindo – he died clasping my photo to his breast. This was a consecrated man, very conscious, with an unfailing dedication, and all the parts of his being well organized around the psychic. The day he was going to leave his body little M. was meditating next to the Samadhi when suddenly she had a vision: she saw all the flowers of the tree next to the Samadhi (those yellow flowers I have called 'Service') gathering themselves together to form a big bouquet, and rising, rising straight up. And in her vision these flowers were linked with the image of N.D.. She ran quickly to their house and – he was dead.

I only knew about this vision later, but on my side, when he left, I saw his whole being gathered together, well united, thoroughly homogenous, in a great aspiration, and rising, rising without dispersing, without deviating, straight up to the frontier of what Sri Aurobindo has called 'the higher hemisphere,' there where Sri Aurobindo in his Supramental action presides over earth. And he melted into that light.

Some time before his heart attack he said to his children: the gown is old, it must be thrown away.

Silence

But people are so ignorant! They make such a fuss over death, as if it were the end – this word 'death' is so absurd! I see it as simply passing from one house into another or from one room to another; you take one simple step, you cross the threshold, and there you are on the other side – and then you come back.

Have I told you about the experience I had the day I suddenly found myself in Sri Aurobindo's home in the subtle physical? Well, it's as if I took a step and entered a far more concrete world than the physical – more concrete because things contain more truth. I spent a good while there with Sri Aurobindo and then, when it was over, I took another step and I found myself back here ... slightly dumbfounded. It took me quite some time to regain my bearings here, because it was this world that seemed unreal to me, not the other.

But it's simply that – you take a step, and you enter another room. And when you live in your soul there is a continuity, because the soul remembers, it keeps the whole memory; it remembers all occurrences, even outer occurrences, all the outer movements it has been associated with. So it's a continuous, uninterrupted movement, here and there, from one room to another, from one house to another, from one life to another.

People are so ignorant! That's what irritates those who have passed to the other side – people don't understand, they shoo them away: 'What does he want? Why does he bother me? He's DEAD!'

Mother's Agenda, 24.6.61

Most people are afraid of the invisible

There's a curious thing: most people are afraid of the invisible, to such a point that when someone is dead (someone they loved when he was alive), they don't want to see him after his death!

I've had one more example today. It's a woman who was murdered; I immediately took care of her psychic, it went away there. But a part of her vital stayed on, and she stayed on with them *(the family)*. I thought they would be happy - they were scared! ... It's a curious thing. So I said, "Oh, it's very simple *(laughing)*, I'll take her with me, like that...." You know, I have a crowd around me - it's not cumbersome in the least.

I don't understand. What is it? ... I don't understand, because even when I was small and knew nothing (I didn't even know it really existed), I was never afraid of invisible things.... Why? ... someone without a body is less cumbersome than someone with a body - someone with a body takes up room, needs room; someone who's not alive doesn't take up any room, he may be there without hampering in the least .... So is it only the appearance people love? the body? ... Strange.

But I've had hundreds of examples. Someone who, eight days earlier, was friendly with a person; the person dies, and eight days later, when he sees her in his dream, he drives her away brutally! ... It happened several times.

It's strange.

Maybe because they're scared of misleading appearances - things of that sort? But one should be able to feel the difference ... (*Mother feels the air*).

Mother's Agenda, 6.9.69

Why be afraid of the dead?

I saw T. She told me about her mother's departure, and said you talked to her about a certain experience you had had with her mother during her whole period of coma or "unconsciousness"?

Yes.

And she would like you to tell your experience again.

You know, I can never tell the same experience twice. It came (it wasn't my intention to tell her all that; my intention was to say a word or two, "All is well"), then it came, and so I spoke. But once it has come out, it's over. I don't even remember what I told her. One thing I know. It's that I deliberately (I don't know if this is what she understood), I deliberately wanted her mother's departure to take place in the most harmonious possible conditions, with the least possible wastage, so she may retain the COMPLETE fruit of her passage in life, and ... What I did in reality (but this I didn't tell her), from the moment I got the news of her stroke (it was an apoplectic seizure), was to put her in a bath of the Lord. I kept her like this (*gesture of enfolding*). So, as for me, I knew first of all that if she was

136

to be cured, she would recover quickly enough, and that if she didn't recover, it would show it was really time for her to go, but then she would go with ... her body benefitting, so to speak, the substance benefitting from the whole profit from physical life, and with her inner being in the best conditions. Of course, the inner being in the best conditions is the case for everyone, for all those who pass away here (but I generally don't have the opportunity to let the inner being go out slowly, you understand). I saw ... you know that when Sri Aurobindo left, we kept him for five days; I saw how it happened. I told you, while I stood beside him, it came out of his body and entered mine, and it was so material that there was a friction – the body felt the friction of the Force coming in. And I saw (of course, in that case it was quite different, tremendous, but for everybody it's like that), I saw this: for the departure to be as harmonious as possible, it should take place like that, according to an inner RHYTHM, with the Presence (which is both a protection and a help), the Presence of the divine Force. So I put her in that Presence. And even (I don't know if she told you), when her brother, who is a doctor, came, he declared with their usual overweening confidence, "Oh, she'll be gone before tomorrow noon." I didn't say anything, remained quiet. Naturally, three more days went by. And even he was forced to acknowledge that there was something there he didn't understand.

What did she tell you?

She told me you had had a special experience with her mother, in the sense that the consciousness of the cells, the material consciousness of her body's cells, was able to leave along with the inner being, it wasn't lost.

Yes, but that is the NORMAL thing.

It's the normal thing. But then, it takes time. And the result is that the whole benefit the cells got isn't lost.

Yes, here, they hurry to burn people, that's terrible.

Oh! ... But she was buried. Oh, I know that. I know, I saw two or three cases here, people who were conscious – it was horrible for them, frightful, frightful.

There was the case of C. He had learned to go out of his body, he knew how to do it: he would go about and see things; he would see, note things, and come back into his body. Then, when he was operated on, the doctors didn't take the necessary precautions and the heart couldn't withstand the shock of the operation: five days later, it was over. But he was in the habit of going out, so he went out and came to me (that's how I knew it before they came to tell me he was "dead"). But he wasn't at all aware of being dead: he had gone out of his body as he used to, and he came to me. He was with me. So then, it was quite fine, he remained peaceful. Then, at a certain point ... (he died in hospital, and naturally, at that time nobody listened to me: they burned him much too soon – it would have been too soon anyway, because in his case, precisely because he had that practice, much precaution and time would have been required; but it was all rushed through), then all of a sudden, when they burned him (I didn't even know the time of the cremation), he suddenly came into my room, you know, appalled ... appalled, crying, miserable: "But I am dead! I didn't know I was dead, but I am dead and they've burned me, they've burned me!..." Oh ... it was horrible, horrible. So I calmed him down, told him to stay there, be calm, be with me, and that I would find him another body. And for a long, long time I had him consciously near me. Then I taught him to reincarnate – it was all done in detail. So I know.

The same thing with N.S.. In his case also ... He had fallen on his head and fractured it (he fell in a faint in the street, that's how he died). He was taken to the hospital. But he went out and came to me right away (and so I knew: when I was told the accident had happened, I already knew something had happened because he had come to me). I kept him there, put him to rest, and he was quite peaceful – quite peaceful. They didn't even consult me about the time when he should be burned or anything (of course, a family of doctors!). Then, suddenly, brrt! (*gesture of bursting*) he went out of my atmosphere abruptly, like that. And no more sign of him.... It took me DAYS to recontact him – and that was the shock he had when they burned his body. It took me days to find him again, put him back to rest, gather him together. And one part had disappeared; his whole consciousness didn't return, because a part of his most material consciousness, of the material vital, must have been thrown out by the shock. I know it, because Albert's father was operated on (it was more than a year later, maybe two), and when he was chloroformed, he suddenly saw N.S. in front of him (of course, even a part can take on the appearance of the whole being; Sri Aurobindo explained that, it's like a photograph). He saw N.S., and N.S. asked him news of his family, news of his wife, news of his children, and he told him, "I worry about them." It must have been the part tied to his family, which must have been separated from the rest of his being: when he came to me, he was complete, but afterwards, I don't know what happened (*gesture of bursting under the shock*). And it was so concrete that when Albert's father was woken up again, he said aloud, "But why are you cutting short my conversation with N.S.?" That's how they found out. He told them, "But I was talking with N.S., why have you interrupted my conversation?"

So they found out.

There.

(*Sujata:*) *Mother, I too saw N.S.*

When?

It was the year he died, but months later. Less than a year later: eight or nine months. I saw him, he had come to my house (it was in the night, in dream), he was in our house, standing near the door, and I went to see him. But someone who was near me said, "But he's dead!" And that gave poor N.S. such a shock, he was in pain. So I took him with me, made him stretch out on my bed. V. was there, and I sent her to inform you.

All that in dream?

All that in dream. I calmed him down, then told V. to go and see you.

But that division, that separated part came about when they burned him. Until then, I had kept him complete, and would have made him pass into the psychic as I do with everyone, peacefully, smoothly, without difficulty. But brrt! (*same gesture of bursting*) It's a frightful shock, you know! They put the fire in the mouth first.... It's ... Oh, the way men behave with each other – I have SEEN all that, I have SEEN it.... It's such a frightful, frightful thing!

And to think that ... It has happened not once or twice but hundreds of times that people who loved someone (they loved their father or brother, or their mother), as soon as that person is dead, if they see him in a dream or vision, they get terribly frightened and try to chase him away! .... Why?... If I ask them why, it's such a spontaneous movement in them that they can't answer me. They can't, they find it so natural that they are surprised I should ask the question.

That's what I said to T. (I don't think she understood), I told her that there isn't so much difference between what people call "life" and what they call "death"; the difference is very small, and grows still smaller when you go into the problem in depth and in all the details. People always make a *clean cut* between the two – it's quite stupid: some living are already half dead, and many dead are VERY alive.

Mother's Agenda, 4.10.67

140

Why death happens?

The central will accepts dissolution.

It happens like this: the central will of the physical being abdicates its will to hold all the cells together. That's the first phenomenon. The central will accepts dissolution. But everything doesn't just scatter all at once – it takes a long time.

What precedes death is accepting to cease the centralization in the form for some reason or other. I have noticed that one of the strongest reasons (one of them, very strong) is a sense of irreparable disharmony. Another is a sort of disgust at carrying on the effort of coordination.

There are, in fact, innumerable reasons, but there is a sort of effort of cohesion and harmonization, and what inevitably precedes death (unless it's caused by a violent accident) is that, for one reason or another, or for no reason, that will to maintain cohesion abdicates.

Mother's Agenda, 3.6.68

A psychic will to die.

There are two things. Death, it doesn't at all understand what we mean by that, the importance we attach to it – but not at all. And then money, to this consciousness, is buffoonery: this system of money, the invention of this system, which prevents you from doing anything unless you pull out a banknote, to it, really it's buffoonery. Strange, I suddenly realize that the psychic being (*dominating gesture behind*) ... the psychic being is almost like a witness, it's a witness to the whole evolution of things, and it KNOWS (it understands the deeper reasons, it knows how things are). It's in the body that this Consciousness is so active, and so, every time the body goes on with the little habits from the time when there was a mind and a vital, really it feels it as buffoonery. And the attitude with regard to money is like ... Death, food and money: this Consciousness feels those are the three "awesome" things in human life, that human life revolves around those three things - eating, (*laughing*) dying, and having money – and to it, the three are ... they are passing inventions which derive from a wholly transitory state that doesn't correspond to anything very deep or very permanent. That's its attitude. And then, it teaches the body to be otherwise.

It tolerates food, provided it doesn't take up too big a place and isn't too cumbersome or too important; it says, "Very well, that's the way you're built, too bad for you, you've got to eat." (*Mother laughs*)

And then, death ... Just yesterday (yesterday afternoon), I had an example. An accident took place, have you heard about it? They're really wondering how it happened. As for me, I INSTANTLY saw that there was in the girl a psychic will (which she wasn't conscious of: she only felt an unease), but there was a psychic will to die (why? I don't know, I haven't yet seen why). That was clear.

And how everything was arranged to favour that, it's almost miraculous (you don't talk about it because people will say you're going mad if you call such a misfortune "miraculous"). But habitually, all those who go into the swimming pool have to put their name down when they go out (that's the rule). Yesterday, the man who kept the register had asked to go to Madras at 6, so he wasn't there and no one's name was noted down, and so they didn't know ... Things like that. She went to see the group's captain and told her, "I am tired, I don't feel well, I want to go;" the captain said, "Yes, yes, you can go." (Of course, it was foolish not to check that she had left; the captain was busy and just thought, "All right, she's leaving.") The girl was then at the shallow end of the pool – impossible to get drowned there, unless you do it quite deliberately (they found her at the other end). But the pool was full of people – nobody saw anything. You see, everything was arranged just to ... force her to die. Every precaution is in place, and not one worked. And as soon as they told me the news of the accident, as soon as I was told, I immediately looked, and I saw, in the place of her psychic, a peaceful will, like this (*Mother stretches out her two arms in an immutable gesture*). They were working hard: they worked for hours; first they took all the water out (they know how to do that), they drained the body of the water, then started working - tractions and all that to try to make her breathe again – they worked for hours (they were ready to work the whole night), they did all they could. And the psychic was like this (*same gesture*), that is, immutable, determined. But she didn't know (that she was going to die): it came through her vital to reach her, and she felt quite ill at ease, she said, "Oh, I want to go out." So they told her, "Yes, that's right, you should go...." And because she had said that, naturally no one was worried when they didn't see her (no one had put their names down, so they couldn't check); it's only when they found her clothes ... She had been under water for over an hour.

This Consciousness was so conscious of the movement in everyone, of every reaction, it was extraordinary! And it's this Consciousness that saw this, that showed me this: a psychic like this (*same immutable gesture*), like an irrevocable decision. And for this Consciousness, you understand, it's like someone who decides to move to a new house, or to a new room, or even to change clothes .... "Why do you make so much, so much fuss about that?"

I haven't said any of this, because ... I haven't said anything to anyone.

Silence

Last year, you remember, there was a boy who drowned at Gingee: that was with P. (the group's captain); and this little one, it was with B., R's sister (also a captain). So I looked: outwardly, they are vitally very strong and very egocentric, which would be the external, material reason that allows the accident to take place - that is, no intuition of other's needs or state: no contact, they're like this (*gesture closed in on oneself*), but with an inner solidity on which the psychic was leaning, for both of them (the two captains).

The other one too (the boy who drowned in the pond) wanted to go, but in his case it was very interesting: I saw Sri Aurobindo

143

come and fetch him under water, and Sri Aurobindo said, "He will be born in the family" (he came back in a child), "he will come back in the first child to be born in the family." And this girl, I don't know yet what will happen, but her psychic being WANTED to go (for some reason or other).

Mother's Agenda, 3.5.69

Man gives a great importance to life and death...

Also, there's a kind of demonstration from the general point of view. Man gives a great importance to life and death - for him there's a great difference, death is a rather capital event(!). And I am shown to what extent the disequilibrium which, in circumstances, results in what people call "death" (which is death only quite apparently), how the two things, so to speak, are constantly there: this all-containing Harmony which is the very essence of Life, and this ... division (it's a sort of division, yes, of fragmentation), this fragmentation, this APPARENT, UNREAL division, which has an ARTIFICIAL existence, and which is the cause of death - how the two are interwoven in such a way that you can go from one to the other at any time and on any occasion. And it's not at all as people think, that there needs to be something "serious" - it's not that, it can happen with the most futile thing! It's simply being here or being there *(with the edge of her hand, Mother very slightly tilts to one side and to the other)*, and that's all. So you are here *(slight tilt to the left)* and remain here: it's over; you are here, and then you are there *(gesture in between the two)*, you are here one second, then you are there: it makes for a life with sufferings and troubles - all kinds of things. And being there *(slight tilt to the right)* is perpetual Life, absolute Power and ... you can't even call it "peace," it's ... something immutable. And at the same time, everything is there: this state and that state are both there. And man makes a more or less clumsy mixture of the two things.

But a few seconds of the true state in its purity and there's ... an awesome power. Only ... it's still far, far away.

Mother's Agenda, 30.4.69

144

If it's death, well, may Your Will be done.

Generally, it comes like that, that discomfort I mentioned; so immediately, the body surrenders – surrenders as if saying (it doesn't say, but anyway it's as if): "If it's death, well, may Your Will be done." You understand, total surrender. So then, when the surrender is... (if it's more or less effective, I don't know), sometimes a clarity comes, an understanding, a SELF-EVIDENCE of everything – a truly remarkable state. But it doesn't last. The least thing disrupts it.

Long silence

I know.... The body feels that if it could surrender TOTALLY – have no independent existence, no personal effort, no personal will ... insofar as that's possible, everything is fine. But this is a tension and a fatigue that are becoming absolutely unbearable, so... Generally, that's what brings about death, it's the fatigue of the tension of life. Last night again, it was like that.... It's becoming so, so strong that I ... I was like this (*gesture of surrender*) and the body gave itself in order to ... (how can I put it?), we can't say to "disappear", but like this (*gesture of fusion and surrender*). So I was lying on my bed as if ... I might say ... I can't say "ready to die" because there was no will either to die or not to die, but it was like this: without resistance, absolutely without resistance. So then, what happened? I don't know, hours went by, and then I woke up – it isn't "sleep", yet it was something like sleep.

Last night.

In the morning, it wasn't more difficult than usual – it wasn't much easier, but not more difficult than usual.

Whenever the body manages not to think about itself (I don't know how to explain this, because it's not a "thought"), not to be conscious of itself, then things are better.

Mother's Agenda, 13.5.70

145

The consciousness at the time of death

When they're in too much of a hurry to burn them, sometimes they burn them alive! ... They should wait.

K. left his body. The operation had been extraordinarily, almost miraculously successful - one of those dreadful operations where they extract part of your body. He was quite all right for four days afterwards, then everything went wrong.

During the operation and just afterwards, I had simply put the Force on him, as I always do in such cases, so that everything would turn out for the best. Then a few days ago, during my japa, a kind of order came - a very clear order - to concentrate on him so that he would be conscious of his soul and able to leave under the best conditions. And I saw that the concentration worked wonderfully: it seems that during his last days he was ceaselessly repeating Ma-Ma-Ma - even while he was in a semi-coma.

And the concentration grew stronger and stronger. The day before yesterday it became very, very powerful, and yesterday morning, around half past noon, it pulled me inward; he came to me in a kind of sleep, a conscious sleep, and I even said almost aloud, 'Oh, K.!'

It lasted fifteen minutes; I was completely within, inside, as if to receive him.

But there is something interesting: when I went down at 2 p.m., I found the family had come to inform me that they had been notified by telephone that he had died at 11:45 a.m. Myself, I saw him come at 12:30.

So you see, the outer signs ... It's not the first time I've noticed this - the doctors observe all the outer signs, then they declare you dead, but you're still in your body!

In other words, he was still in his body.

So it's probably during this period that people are 'resuscitated', as they say. It must be during this period, for they have not left their bodies, they are not really dead, though the heart may give every appearance of having stopped.

So K. left his body at around half past noon, and officially it was at 11:45. Forty-five minutes later, in other words.

And it takes place very gently, very gently (when it's done right), very gently, very gently, smoothly, without any shock.

So this morning they're burning him.

When they're in too much of a hurry to burn them, sometimes they burn them alive! ... They should wait.

For there's a consciousness of the form, a life of the form. There's a consciousness, a consciousness in the form assumed by the cells. That takes SEVEN DAYS to come out. So sometimes the body makes abrupt movements when burned - people say it's mechanical. It's not mechanical, I know it's not.

I know it. I know that this consciousness of the form exists since I have actually gone out of it. Once, long back, I was in a so-called cataleptic state, and after awhile, while still in this state, the body began living again; that is, it was capable of speaking and even moving (it was Théon who gave me this training). The body managed to get up and move. And yet, everything had gone out of it!

Once everything had gone out, it naturally became cold, but the body consciousness manages to draw a little energy from the air, from this or that ... And I spoke in that state. I spoke - I spoke very well, and besides, I recounted all I was seeing elsewhere.

So I don't like this habit of burning people very much.

I think they do it here (apart from entirely sanitary considerations in the case of people who have died from nasty diseases), here in India, mainly because they are very afraid of all these little entities that come from desires, impulses - things which are dispersed in the air and which make 'ghosts' and all kinds of things. All desires, all attachments, all those things are like pieces that break off (each one goes its own way, you see), then these pieces gain strength in the surrounding atmosphere, and when they can fasten on to someone, they vampirize him. Then they keep on trying to satisfy their desires.

The world, the terrestrial atmosphere, is full of filth.

And people here are much more sensitive than in Europe because they are much more interiorized, so they are conscious of all these little entities, and naturally they're afraid. And the more afraid they are, the more they're vampirized!

I think that many of these entities are dispersed by fire - that creates havoc.

I know one person, a boy who died here, who was burned before he had left! He had a weak heart, and not enough care was taken - that is, they probably should not have operated on him. He was our engineer. He died in the hospital. Not a serious operation, an appendicitis, but his heart could not take up its natural movement.

But as he was accustomed to going out of his body, he didn't know! He even used to make experiments - he would go out, circle around in his room, see his body from outside, observe the difference between the subtle physical and the material physical, etc. So he didn't know. And it's only when they burned his body...

I tried to delay the moment, but he was in the hospital, so it was difficult. I was in my room when they burned his body, and then suddenly I saw him arrive - sobbing - saying, 'But ... But I'm dead. I DIDN'T WANT to die! Why am I dead, I DIDN'T WANT to die!' It was dreadful. So I kept him and held him against me to quiet him down.

He remained there for years.

And whenever we used to have meetings to decide on the construction of something or on repairs to be made, for example, I always felt him there and he influenced those who were present.

He wanted to live again; I managed to give him the opportunity. He was very conscious; the child isn't yet so.

But people are such fools, they are so ignorant!...

Mother's Agenda, 28.5.60

When the accident occurred, he came to me...

As you know, N.S. has left his body. It was the result of an accident (he had a weak heart, and he worried about it). He took a fall, probably because he fainted, and fractured his skull: "loss of consciousness" due to cerebral hemorrhage (that's modern science speaking!). When the accident occurred, he came to me (not in a precise form, but in a state of consciousness I immediately recognized), and stayed here motionless, in complete trust and blissful peace - motionless in every state of being, absolutely ... *(gesture of surrender)* total, total trust: what will be, will be; what is, is. No questions, not even a need to know. A cosy peace ... a *great ease.*

They tried, fought, operated: no movement, nothing moved. Then one day they declared him dead (by the way, according to doctors, when the body dies the heart beats on faintly for a few seconds; then it stops and it's all over). In his case, those faint beats (not strong enough to pump blood) continued for half an hour - the kind of heartbeats typical of the trance state. (They all seem to be crassly ignorant! But anyway, it doesn't matter.) And they all said, even the doctors, "Oooh, he must be a great yogi, this only happens to yogis!" I have no idea what they mean by that. But I do know that although those heartbeats aren't strong enough to pump blood through the body (thus putting the body into a cataleptic state), they do suffice to maintain life, and that's how yogis can remain in trance for months on end. Well, I don't know what type of doctors they are (probably very modern), but they're ignorant of this fact. Anyway, according to them he had those pulsations for half an hour (normally they last a few seconds). All right. Hence their remarks. And he was here the whole while, immutable. Then suddenly I felt a kind of shudder; I looked - he was gone. I was busy and didn't note the time, but it was in the afternoon, that's all I know. Later I was told that they had decided to cremate him, and had done so at that time.

The violence of the accident had brutally exteriorized him, but when it happened he must have been thinking of me with trust. He came and didn't budge - he never knew what was happening to his body. He didn't know he was dead! And if....

Then and there I said to myself, "This habit of cremating people is appallingly brutal!" (They put the fire in the mouth first.) He didn't know he was dead and that's how he learned it! ... From the reaction of the life of the form in the body.

Even when the body is in a thoroughly bad condition, it takes at least seven days for the life of the form to leave it. And for someone practicing yoga, this life is CONSCIOUS. So you burn people a few hours after the doctors have declared them dead, but the life of the form is every inch alive and, in those who have practiced yoga, conscious.

It made me a bit....

Given the state he was in, it made NO difference to him whether he was dead or alive; that's what was interesting! He remained in a blissful, trusting, peaceful state and I probably would have gently led him either to the psychic world or elsewhere, according to the indication I received as to what he had to do. He would never have known he was dead. (*Later, Mother commented*: "This experience is interesting. He would have been able to EXIST in a psychic state [psychically, of course, one is immortal], he would have existed not knowing that he was dead ... if they hadn't burned him.")

This opened a door for me. (*Recall the conversation of June 12:* "I don't know whether I am dead or alive.... A type of life vibration which is completely independent of.... I can't say 'I am alive,' it's something else entirely.")

Because they cremated him he was abruptly *(Mother violently shudders)* and violently thrown into contact with the destruction of the body's form. ("I mean a SUBTLE form," Mother clarified, "it's the body's subtle form.") It must have been the life of the form; when hurled so brutally out of the body, the life of the form must have thrown itself at him! So of course....

Silence

I immediately said to myself, "But he was still existing, living, having the experience, absolutely INDEPENDENT of his body - he didn't need his body to have his experience." And with my protection and knowledge I could have put him either in a place of rest or, if need be, in touch with another body - and that would have been the end of it. Now, of course, everything is disrupted and we have to wait for things to calm down. (*One week later, Mother added*: "It has worked out: he has gone to the psychic domain for a while - I think it's only for a while - to concentrate.")

But it is possible to die without knowing you are dead.

And to retain full consciousness - he was totally conscious and blissful.

I find that important, an important experience.

I haven't told anyone what happened when they cremated him, because it would have made them all quite upset and miserable. I said only that he came to me. So don't say a word; they mustn't know. Not that it's irreparable, but still, it's not a pleasant experience.

But it came as if to put me in contact with this possibility.

Mother's Agenda, 4.7.62

He has put Himself in the role of spectator and He's watching Himself.

Actually, if you look at things closely, you're forced to conclude that the Lord is acting out a tremendous comedy for Himself, that the Manifestation is a comedy He's playing with and for Himself!

He has put Himself in the role of spectator and He's watching Himself. And to watch Himself, He has to accept the notion of time and space – otherwise He can't watch Himself! And immediately the whole comedy begins. But it's a comedy and nothing more!

And we're the puppets, eh! That's why we take it so seriously. But as soon as we stop being puppets, we realize it's a comedy.

For some people it's a real tragedy, too.

Yes, because we make it tragic. WE make it tragic.

152

I've been focusing on this lately. I've been looking at the difference between similar events in the lives of human beings and the lives of animals. If you identify with animals, you clearly see that they don't take things tragically at all – except for those which have come into contact with man. (But then they're not in their natural state; it's a transitional state, they are beings in transition between animal and man.) And naturally the first things they pick up from man are his defects – that's always what's easiest to pick up! And then they make themselves unhappy... for nothing.

So many things, so many things.... Human beings have made an appalling tragedy out of death. And I saw, with all these recent experiences, I saw how many, many poor human beings have been destroyed by the very people they loved the most! Under the pretext that they were dead.

People give them a very bad time.

Destroyed?

Yes, burned. Or shut up in a box without air and light – while FULLY CONSCIOUS. And just because they can no longer express themselves, people say they are "dead". They don't waste any time declaring them dead! But they are conscious. They are conscious. Imagine someone who can no longer speak or move – according to human laws, he is "dead". He is dead but he is conscious. He is conscious, so he sees the people around him: some of them are weeping, some of them are... if he's a bit clairvoyant, he also sees that some of them are rejoicing. And then he sees himself put into a box, sees the lid nailed down, shutting him in: "Ah, now it's all over, they're going to cover me with earth!" Or he's taken over there (to the cremation ground), and then it's fire in the mouth – FULLY conscious.

I have lived this in recent days. I have seen it. Last night or the night before, I spent at least two hours in a world – the subtle physical world – where the living mingle with the dead with no sense of difference, it makes absolutely no difference there. For instance, when Mridu was in her body I used to see her at night maybe once a year (maybe not even that much). For years she was utterly nonexistent in my consciousness... but since she left her body, I see her almost every night! There she is, just as she was, you know (*rotund gesture*), but no longer troubled, that's all. No longer troubled. And there were both living and... what we call the "living" and the "dead" – they were both there together, eating together, moving around together, having fun together; and all in a lovely, tranquil light – pleasant, very pleasant. "There!" I thought, "and humans have drawn a sharp line, saying, 'Now he's dead!'" Dead! And what really takes the cake is the way they treat the body like an unconscious object, and it's still conscious!

It's treated like an object: "Now then! Let's get rid of this just as quickly as we can: it's a nuisance and it gets in the way." And even those who feel the most sorrow don't want to see it; it's too painful for them.

Mother's Agenda, 12.10.62

Then I put him to rest and sent him to join the rest of his being.

I've had a very interesting experience (not personal). Did you know Benjamin *(an old disciple who had just died)*? ... His psychic being had left him quite some time ago and, as a result, to the surface consciousness he seemed a bit deranged - he wasn't deranged but diminished. And he lived, as I said, out of habit. The physical consciousness still held a minimum of vital and mind and he lived out of habit. But the remarkable thing is that sometimes, for a few seconds, he would live admirably, in full light, while at other times he couldn't even control his gestures. Then he left altogether: all the accumulated energy dwindled little by little, little by little, and whatever remained left his body. It was just on his birthday, on December 30th (the night of December 30th) he left. So they did as is always done: they cleaned his room, took out the furniture. Since then, there had been no sign of him. Yesterday evening, after dinner

154

(which is about the same time he left twelve days ago), I was in concentration, resting, when suddenly here comes a very agitated Benjamin who tells me, "Mother, they've taken all the furniture out of my room! What am I to do now!?" I told him gently, "Do not fret, you don't need anything any more." Then I put him to rest and sent him to join the rest of his being.

Which means it took twelve days for all his elements to form again. You see, they burned his body. (He was Christian, but his family - his wife is alive and his brother too - found it less costly to let us handle it than to bury him as a Christian! So they had him cremated.) We cremated him, but I demanded a certain interval of time *(before the cremation, so as to give the consciousness time to come out)*, although in his case it was really a gradual exhaustion and nothing much remained in his body; nonetheless, even then the consciousness is flung out of the cells violently - it took twelve days to form again. It wasn't his soul (it had already left) but the spirit of his body that came to me, the body consciousness gathered in a well-dressed, neat Benjamin with his hair neatly brushed. He was quite trim when he came to me, just as he would have been in life: he always wanted to be well-groomed and impeccable to see me, that was his way. It took twelve days to gather together because I didn't see to it (I can do it in a few hours but only if I see to it), but in his case, his soul having been at rest for a long time, it didn't matter much. So over twelve days it took form again and when he was ready *(laughing)*, he came to reoccupy his room! ... And there was no furniture left, nothing! I found that very funny.

And he had been living for more than a year, almost two years, I think, just out of a habit of living.

There is also here the sister of the old portly doctor, she is (I think) five or six years older than I - she is getting on for ninety. She has been dying away too, for several months. The doctors (who don't know the first thing in these matters) had declared she would die after a few days. "Wait a little," I told them, "this woman knows how to enter a state of rest, she has a very peaceful consciousness - it will last long, it may last for years." She is in bed, she can't move much, but ... she lives. She too lives out of habit.

In reality, the body should be able to last MUCH LONGER than human beings think. They knock it about: as soon as someone is unwell, they drug or knock his body about, they take away that kind of calm vegetative serenity that can make it last a very long time. The way trees take a very long time to die.

Interesting.

Mother's Agenda, 12.1.63

It takes QUITE A WHILE for the consciousness to come out slowly!

How they treat those poor dead!...

Naturally, they rushed to cremate him; they asked me candidly (because his nephew was coming but not before the next morning, that is, a little less than twenty-four hours after M.'s death – nearly twenty hours), they asked me, "Should we keep him or not?" I answered, "It depends. If you ask me as far as HE is concerned, certainly the longer you keep him the better." Then I see eyes open wide, a mouth open wide – don't understand anything! I told them, "It takes QUITE A WHILE for the consciousness to come out slowly! Otherwise, when you burn him, it's pushed out violently, it gives a terrible shock."

To tell the truth, people burn the dead in that way to destroy the vital, I am sure of it. The idea is not to have *any ghosts*.

A little before his death he had asked me for a new name. He had nearly died twice, but he was saved (the doctors were sure he would die), he was saved by his faith; he had such faith, such an irresistible faith that twice it pulled him through: he was paralyzed, couldn't see any more, it was terrible. And twice all his faculties came back (his eyes weren't too good, but anyway he could talk and move around). The third time, he wanted to get completely cured, because he was a businessman and had made a resolve to earn ten lakhs of rupees for me (he had already

156

given me four lakhs in the past, but he wanted to give me ten).
So he absolutely wanted to live, but as he found himself not too
well (he was quite deteriorated!), he called for one of those
kaviraj (you know, those self-styled doctors), who finished him
off: he couldn't eat or sleep any more. And the "doctor" went
on telling him, "You're much better"! While the poor man was
sitting up all night in a chair.... Finally, he was rushed to the
hospital and died there. And the day of his death, about an hour
later, I was informed that his son (he's not a child, he's a man)
absolutely HAD to see me immediately. It was the time when
I don't see people, but I said "all right" (I felt there was
something to it), I said "all right" and went to receive him. It
was 11:00 a.m. (I think he died at 9:30 a.m.). I go there (I don't
remember if it was in the morning or early in the afternoon,
anyhow it was very soon after his death), I sit down, the son is
ushered in, and along with him comes a small boy, no taller than
this (*gesture*), all golden, joyous, alive, happy!... And he rushed
to me. He stayed like that, leaning against me, quite still. And
how he laughed! How happy he was!

It was M., his psychic being.

Ever so lovely! All luminous – luminous with a golden light
– and so happy, so glad! Like a baby, no bigger than this
(*gesture*). Waving his arms and legs about, so happy! He stayed
there – stayed put. So naturally, I received him and did the
needful. I've seen thousands of cases, you know, but it's the
first time I've seen that! And he had a remarkable knowledge,
because in order not to risk any hitch, he clung to his son and
urged him to come to me so as to make sure of reaching me
without mishap, without any interference from the adverse
forces, from currents and all sorts of things. He clung to his
son, who was quite unaware of it, except that something in
him WANTED him to come to me. And the poor son was
crying; I told him, "Don't worry, he is very happy"! (*Mother
laughs*)

And lovely! A lovely thing. The sight of it filled me with joy
– so happy, so happy, he seemed to be saying, "At last I am
with you! I won't budge now, no one can take me away." This

small. I told you the story of the other one who came to be operated on and died (that makes two in a row, among our best workers). The other one had an important government position and did us some incredible services (he was a very intelligent man and had been Chief Justice for a very long time), he was very helpful and full of faith and devotion. This one (M.) had even promised to lend some money, but he died just before – a few days before he was due to give it! But the first one was a conscious, highly mentalized being, with a very well-formed mental being; he knew a lot and he told me, "I am very conscious and now I know that I am fully alive and fully conscious, so I don't want an impotent body that constantly requires someone to nurse it or move it around. I prefer to change." He asked me to find him a good one(!). This one didn't ask to take a new body, but the last thing he said (afterwards, he was paralyzed) was: *I must live, because I want to give ten lakhs of rupees to the Mother*. And he left with that – so an appropriate body has to be found.

But this one (M.) knew very little, he wasn't an intellectual, he was a man of action, very psychic – very much so! Lovely, oh, lovely! He was like a little child, naked, of course, a baby this big, with small arms, small legs – dancing about, he was glad, laughing and laughing, he was happy. And all luminous. I immediately told his son (he did a "pranam" and rose with his eyes full of tears), I told him, *"Don't weep, he is now where he wants to be and perfectly at rest."* I didn't tell him the story – he wouldn't have understood a thing!

Mother's Agenda, 27.7.63

She spent the last moments of her life with me.

I remember, the very day when Janina (a *woman disciple of Polish origin, who was a painter*) died (she died around 6 in the morning, I think), around 4 in the morning, something made me suddenly take interest in this question: What will the new form be like? What will it be? I was looking at man and at the animal, and then I saw that there would be a far greater difference between man and the new form than between man and the animal. I began to see certain things, and it so happened that Janina was there (in her thought, but a material enough and very concrete thought). It was very interesting (it lasted a long time, nearly two hours), because I saw all the timidity of human conceptions, while she had made contact with something: it wasn't an idea but a sort of contact (*with a future reality*). And I had the sense of a more plastic Matter, more full of Light, much more directly responsive to the Will (the higher Will), and with such a plasticity that it could respond to the Will by taking on variable and changing forms. And I saw some of her own forms, forms that she conceived (rather like those beings who don't have a body as we do, but have hands and feet when they will it, a head when they will it, luminous clothes when they will it - things of that sort), I saw that, and I remember I was congratulating her; I told her, "Yours was a partial but partially very clear perception of one of the forms the new Manifestation will take." And she was very happy; I told her, "You see, you have fully worked for the future." And then, suddenly, I saw a sapphire blue light, pale, very luminous, with something like the shape of a flame (with a rather broad base), and there was a kind of flash - pfft! - and it was gone. She wasn't there anymore. I thought, "Well, that's odd!"

An hour later (I saw that around 6 a.m.; all the rest had lasted about two hours), they told me she was dead. Which means she spent the last moments of her life with me, and then, from me, pfft! went off towards ... a life elsewhere.

It was very abrupt. She was so happy, you know, I told her, "How well you have worked for the future!" And all of a sudden, a sort of flash (a sapphire blue light, pale, very luminous, with the shape of a flame and a rather broad base), pfft! she was gone. And that was just the time when she died.

It's one of the most interesting departures I have seen - fully conscious. And so happy to have participated! ... I myself didn't know why I was telling her, "Yes, you have truly participated in the work for the future, you have put the earth in contact with one of the forms of the new Manifestation."

Mother's Agenda, 11.8.64

Can one have the experience of death without dying?

Surely! You can have the experience in a yogic way, you can even have it materially if ... (*laughing*) if death is brief enough not to give the doctors time to declare you dead!...
They won't understand!
We can answer "Yes," quite simply - so as to tell them, "Mind your own business!"

After death, what is the part of the being that becomes aware that one is dead?

Any part of the being that lives on becomes aware that the body is no longer there! It depends.

How can one say with certainty that the physical body is dead?

Only when it decomposes.

You said, 'Decomposition of the cells often starts before death....' How to control or check the process of disintegration?

(*Mother laughs*) By keeping good health! By taking care to preserve the physical equilibrium. Enough!

Mother's Agenda, 28.9.68

The process is to detach one's consciousness from the body and to concentrate it on the deeper life so as to bring this deeper consciousness into the body.

160

The first question: What should we do in our daily life to halt the process of death?

Well, as Sri Aurobindo has just said, the process is, rather than remain wholly attached to the body, to attach ourselves to the Spirit, and to bring the Spirit down into the body's cells. The process is to detach one's consciousness from the body and to concentrate it on the deeper life so as to bring this deeper consciousness into the body.

Second question: If the sense of 'I-ness' has identified more with the mind in life, is it the same sense of 'I-ness' that has all the experiences after death, that is to say, which retains at the same time the memories of its life? I ask the question with regard to the mind, since after death it remains formed a little longer than the other parts do.

That's not true. It's not true that the mind lasts longer.
    Read it again.

Is it the same sense of 'I-ness' that has all the experiences after death?

No, not at all.
    The psychic consciousness that has identified with the small part of the physical is what comes out of this small physical person. In so far as that consciousness has fashioned one's life, it remembers what it has fashioned, and the memory is closely linked with the psychic consciousness in the past events: whenever the psychic consciousness did not participate in the events, no memory is retained. It's only the psychic consciousness that can continue.
    It's not the mind that retains the memories, that's quite wrong.

Mother's Agenda, 1.2.69

161

The living and the dead

In the subtle physical, as a rule I was always with
Sri Aurobindo.

I saw you last night.

Oh, yes?

Do you remember?...

No.

We were in the subtle physical. I saw lots of people: Purani *(a
departed disciple)* and so on, people who are no longer on earth.
It was in Sri Aurobindo's ... not his house, but his domain.
I saw and did lots of things. There were people who live on
earth and people who no longer do: they were all together.
And at the end (for many details Sri Aurobindo was there, then
he left), at the end I looked at all that, and for the first time in
the subtle physical, I said, "Oh, how insipid and useless your
life is, and flavourless, when you don't think of the Divine."
The experience was so acute! So acute. Then I said (among
the people there, there was Purani, and as I said people who
live on earth), I told them, "On the earth, there is that intensity
of aspiration, but here ... life is so easy, so easy! Look at all
your activities and all that, oh, it has no flavour, because there
isn't that intense need to live for the Divine." And it was so
strong that for hours in the morning it was like that (*gesture of
intense aspiration*). Life anywhere - anywhere, in any part of
the world (of the universe) and in any conditions, even the
most easy and harmonious, is not worth living without this
intensity of aspiration, of the NEED to be divine.
It's the first time.
In the past, when I went to all those regions, there were
always very interesting things; and in the subtle physical, as a
rule I was always with Sri Aurobindo – (last night too) I was

with Sri Aurobindo but he withdrew to a part of his domain and I remained with all the others: they had an easy life, you know, carefree, and all they did seemed so ... meaningless. Why? Why all that, why keep oneself busy, why do all those things if it's not for this aspiration, for this need to be and become the Divine?

But it's the first time, and it lingered on: for hours this morning, I was like this (*gesture of intense aspiration*).

There.

As a result, my impression was that unless the whole universe becomes THAT, well ... what's the use? Everything and anything that isn't the Consciousness, the supreme consciousness, I mean, yes, the supreme and supremely divine consciousness, all the rest ... It's the first time I've felt so intensely the uselessness of all outward activities – their uselessness IN THEMSELVES, like a blossoming, because when there is the divine Play, then the same things become lovely, it all becomes interesting, but in themselves, for themselves, they are NOTHING. It's the first time I have felt that so intensely. Because I felt it in the subtle world (in the material world it's always mixed with all kinds of trouble and effort and difficulty so it's completely different), there, things are absolutely without difficulty, completely harmonious, really, and it was NOTHING. You understand, when Sri Aurobindo was there, it was perfect, but when he withdrew ... flavourless.

And it's the PHYSICAL consciousness that has those experiences at night: the body remains in trance, it's the physical consciousness; it was the physical consciousness, but in a subtle physical released from all difficulties – and it was no better. You know, it was like a reply to the ambition of people here on earth who want life to be pleasant, easy, without difficulties, without conflicts and clashes and diseases and ... they say, "Oh, how charming all would be!" It's not true: if there isn't THAT, empty.

The experience was very interesting.

Mother's Agenda, 6.12.67

Death of death

This gives the cells an intensity in their call for a Power of Eternity...

It's a sort of "overhanging" (it comes to me in English, that's why I have difficulty) of that constant presence of Death or possibility of death. As he *(Sri Aurobindo)* says in *Savitri*, we have a constant companion all the way from the cradle to the grave, we are constantly shadowed by the threat or presence of Death. Well, this gives the cells an intensity in their call for a Power of Eternity which would not be there without that constant threat. Then we understand - we begin to understand very concretely - that all those things are only goads to make the Manifestation progress and grow more intense, more perfect. If the goads are crude, it is because the Manifestation is very crude. As it grows more and more perfect and apt to manifest something ETERNALLY PROGRESSIVE, those very crude methods will give way to more refined ones, and the world will progress without the need for such brutal oppositions. It is only because the world is in infancy and the human consciousness in its very early infancy.

It's a very concrete experience.

So, when the earth no longer needs to die in order to progress, there will be no more death. When the earth no longer needs to suffer in order to progress, there will be no more suffering. And when the earth no longer needs to hate in order to love, there will be no more hatred.

Silence

It is the quickest and most effective method of pulling the creation out of its inertia and leading it on to its blossoming.

Mother's Agenda, 15.5.63

That suggestion of old age ... old age, wear and tear, death.

Yesterday afternoon, I had an experience in relation to a woman who has been in a coma for sixty-five days(!). After fifty or fifty-five days (the whole family was around her, but her son had gone to work), all of a sudden after fifty-five days, because her son had left, she started calling for him, shouting frantically! (*Laughing*) I think they all had a scare.... And the usual stupid remarks: "She was unconscious." I said, "Good God! But why do you say she was unconscious, you know nothing about it... She can't express herself, but she isn't unconscious. She is entirely conscious, only the means of expression are damaged, she can no longer use them." And I made a long speech on the subject, but there was no one to record it and I can never say the same thing twice. It came clearly (Sri Aurobindo was there), and with the absolutely clear picture of what death is.... Now I can't repeat it.

In reality, to put it practically (but that's no longer the thing), what people call "death" is when the instrument of expression - the instrument of connection with the milieu, of expression - has deteriorated to the point where it can no longer be used, and so there comes a moment when the consciousness abandons it.

Probably for all sorts of reasons (there must be different reasons in each case), but the consciousness abandons it because it can no longer be used.

But yesterday it came well; now it's nothing. It was lived. Lived, and so clear, so concrete, so obvious, it was, "But human beings know nothing, nothing, nothing at all!..." Only now it sounds like a platitude.

Silence

The vision was so clear (not vision: lived, the experience), it was so clear that it contained in itself the purpose of the creation. You could see the work of the consciousness to

166

permeate the inconscient and make it progressively more capable of manifesting the consciousness (*gesture like a flower rising out of the earth*), with growing complications, but the complications are the result of the inability of the inconscient - of inconscient matter - which adds one device to another in the hope of reconstructing the supreme Possibility. Then, through all those complications, and as the substance becomes increasingly permeated with consciousness, the need for "devices" will diminish, and we will be able to return to the higher Simplicity.

But all that was lived, seen - seen, and so clear!

Silence

And in each "life", as people call it, that is to say, the use of a portion of matter organized in what we call a body, how that use aims at the greatest possibility of manifestation (reception and manifestation) of the consciousness.

Naturally, this can be done because even in the inconscient, at its very bottom, there is consciousness; but that's philosophy. Yesterday, it was the perfectly concrete and material experience of it all.

And individualization is part of the process, it's a necessity of the process, because it permits a more minute and direct action.

And when Matter is supple enough to be transformed under the action of the consciousness - a CONSTANT transformation - then this need to abandon here something that has become useless, or is in impossible conditions, will no longer exist. That is how it will be possible, for the requirements of the transformation, to have at will a continuity, at least, of existence for a form which was transitional.

But yesterday, the impression was that it *(death)* is now only an old habit, no longer a necessity. It's only because ... First, because the body is still unconscious enough to (how should I put it?), not to "desire," because that's not the word, but to feel the need of complete rest, that is, inertia.

When that is abolished, there is no disorganization that cannot be mended, or at any rate (the field of accidents hasn't been studied, but let's say in the normal course of things) no wear and tear, no deterioration, no disharmony that cannot be mended by the action of the consciousness.

It's only this residue (a considerable one), this residue of inconscient that asks for rest (*gesture of dissolution*). What it calls rest is the state of inertia. That is to say, the refusal to manifest the consciousness. It's no more than that.

There is also that FORMIDABLE collective suggestion ... weighing down. That suggestion of old age ... old age, wear and tear, death ("death", anyway what they call death, which isn't dying - what does "dying" mean? Annulment does not exist, nothing is annulled), but anyway, giving up the form because the form refuses to be transformed (that's nearly what it is) and isn't receptive, it accepts a progressive deterioration because of the formidable weight of the collective suggestion - the habit of millennia: "It's always been like that, it can't be helped." The great argument. Which isn't true, besides.

Mother's Agenda, 21.10.67

These are the two things opposing each other: the effort for progress and transformation, or the brutal and stupid method of smashing everything and starting all over again.

At the very bottom of the thing, two tendencies or two conceptions are confronting each other. The first says, "It's badly done: let's destroy it and we'll begin again," from top to bottom. The other says, "It's not the way it should be: let's transform it." These are the two things opposing each other: the effort for progress and transformation, or the brutal and stupid method of smashing everything and starting all over again, so that it goes on endlessly.

It boils down to the fight between Death and Life; progressive life, more and more divine, and Death, which systematically abolishes all that isn't divine. Because only what is divine escapes it.

But the process is ... endless.

The power of progressive transformation is what must be infused into Matter.

Mother's Agenda, 27.12.67

All you have to do is constantly and always be supple, attentive, and ... responsive to the influence of the Consciousness.

My experience is like this (because now my body no longer obeys the mind or the intelligence at all, no longer at all - it doesn't even understand how that can be done), and it more and more, better and better follows the direction and impulsion of the Consciousness. But then, it sees, almost every minute, the tremendous difference that makes.... For instance, time has lost its value (its rigid value): you can do the same thing in very little time or in much time. Necessities have lost their authority: you can adapt yourself this way, adapt yourself that way. All the laws - those laws that were laws of Nature - have lost all their despotism, if I may say so: it no longer works that way. All you have to do is constantly and always be supple, attentive, and ... responsive to the influence of the Consciousness - the Consciousness in its all-powerfulness - so as to go through all this with extraordinary suppleness.

That is the discovery being made more and more.

And it's wonderful, you know! A wonderful discovery.

It's like a progressive victory over all constraints. So naturally, all the laws of Nature, all the human laws, all habits, all rules, all that grows increasingly supple and finally becomes nonexistent. Yet it is possible to keep a regular rhythm that makes action easier - it's not contrary to this suppleness. But it's a suppleness in the execution, in the adaptation, which comes and changes everything. From the point of view of hygiene, health, organization, from the point

169

of view of the relationship with others, all that has not only lost its aggressiveness (because for it to lose its aggressiveness, all you have to do is to be wise - wise and level-headed and calm), but also its absolutism, its imperative rule: that's entirely gone - gone.

And then, you see: as the process grows more and more perfect - "perfect" means integral, total, leaving nothing behind - it NECESSARILY, inevitably means victory over death. Not that this dissolution of the cells which death involves stops existing, but that it would exist only when necessary: not as an absolute law, but as ONE of the processes, when necessary.

It's mainly all that the Mind has brought in terms of rigidity and absoluteness and near invincibility - that's what is going to disappear. And simply by handing the supreme power over to the Supreme Consciousness.

That may be what the sages of old meant when they spoke of handing the power of Nature or the power of the Prakriti over to the Purusha - handing it from the Prakriti over to the Purusha. Perhaps it was their way of expressing the same thing.

Mother's Agenda, 30.12.67

The Force is there, present as never before.

One needs to have an absolutely transparent sincerity. Lack of sincerity is at present the cause of difficulties.

Insincerity is in all men. There are perhaps a hundred totally sincere men on earth. Man's very nature is what makes him insincere. It's very complicated, for he is constantly cheating with himself, hiding the truth from himself, finding excuses for himself. Yoga is the way to become sincere in all the parts of one's being.

It is difficult to be sincere, but one can at least be mentally sincere – this is what one can demand from Aurovilians.

The Force is there, present as never before; what prevents it from descending and being felt is men's insincerity. The world is steeped in falsehood, all relationships between men have so far been based only on falsehood and deceit. Diplomacy between nations is based on falsehood. They claim they want peace and on the other hand arm themselves. A transparent sincerity in man and between nations will alone permit the coming of a transformed world.

Auroville is the first attempt in the experiment. A new world will be born if men consent to strive for transformation and the search for sincerity – it can be done (see conversation of February 3rd, 1968).

It took millennia to evolve from animal to man; today man, thanks to his mind, can accelerate things and will a transformation towards a man who will be God.

This transformation with the help of the mind, through self-analysis, is a first stage; afterwards, vital impulses must be transformed - which is far more difficult; then, most of all, the physical: each cell of our body will have to become conscious. It is the work I am doing here. It will allow the conquest of death. It's another story; that will be future mankind, perhaps in centuries, perhaps sooner. It will depend on men, on peoples.

Auroville is the first step towards this goal.

Mother's Agenda, 28.2.68

I realized that this experience of the SINGLE Consciousness playing through innumerable forms...

I told her that from the standpoint of the manifestation (I didn't speak about beyond the manifestation), from the standpoint of the manifestation, there is only one thing that is true: Consciousness. And that all the rest is the APPEARANCE of something, but not the thing; that THE thing is Consciousness, and all the rest is a sort of play in which everyone has the illusion of being a personality, but it's an illusion....

While I was speaking, I had the perfectly sincere and spontaneous experience of it. And I realized that this experience of the SINGLE Consciousness playing through innumerable forms...

(Mother breaks off).

But one cannot express that, words can't. While I was speaking, it was that Consciousness which spoke.... And the two experiences together (the children's notes, I read them yesterday evening; as for D., I had seen her in the morning), the two together gave me the detachment (it's not detachment: it's a liberation) from the phenomenon of death in such an absolute way that I was able to look throughout History, far into the past, at the whole human tragedy.... That is to say, death is a natural phenomenon in the creation on earth, but as a means of TRANSITION - I clearly saw why it had become necessary, how, with the human consciousness and mental development, it had been turned into a tragedy, and how it was becoming again merely a means of transition (a clumsy means, we might say), which was now becoming unnecessary again.

There was that whole, overall vision of the history of the creation. It was really interesting. Interesting because ... whew! you felt so free! So free, so peaceful, so smiling! And at the same time, with such a certitude that everything is moving towards a more harmonious, less chaotic, less painful manifestation ... and that there is only one more step to be made in the creation.

Mother's Agenda, 18.5.68

The psychic being materializes itself...

I had an experience which was for me interesting, because it was for the first time. It was yesterday or the day before. I do not remember. X was there just in front of me, and I saw her psychic being, dominating over her by so much (*gesture indicating about twenty centimetres),* taller. It was the first time. Her physical being was small and her psychic being was so much bigger. And it was an unsexed being, neither man nor woman. Then I said to myself (possibly it is always so, I do not know, but here I noticed it very clearly), I said to myself,

"But it is the psychic being, it is that which will materialize itself and become the Supramental being!"

So, one understands. One understands: the psychic being materializes itself... and that gives continuity to evolution. This creation gives altogether the feeling that there is nothing arbitrary, there is a kind of divine logic behind and it is not like our human logic, it is very much superior to ours – but there is one, and that was fully satisfied when I saw this.

And it is precisely the psychic that survives. So, if it materializes itself, it means the abolition of death.

Mother's Agenda, 1.7.70

I mean the physical realization is really a concrete realization.

The body is being taught to exist by the Divine alone, to count on the Divine for everything - absolutely, absolutely everything without exception. There is even a pressure for.... It's only when the consciousness is linked to its utmost to the Divine Consciousness that there's the sense of existence. It has become extraordinarily intense. When the physical gets converted, it will be something SOLID, you know, unalterable - and complete. And so concrete.... The difference between being in the Divine, existing only by Him and for Him, and then being in the ... not in the ordinary consciousness obviously, but just the human consciousness, is so great that the one seems like death compared to the other, it's so.... I mean the physical realization is really a concrete realization.

There is beginning to be such a concentration of energy (oh! it's not there yet, very far from it, but ...), there's a beginning of perception of how things will be. It's ... it's really marvellous. And so powerful! A power and a reality in the consciousness that nothing, absolutely nothing else can have - everything vital or mental and all that seems hazy and unsubstantial. Whereas this is concrete (*Mother clenches her fists*). And so strong!

173

Some problems are still to be solved, but not with words or thoughts. And things come to demonstrate - not just personal things, but also things from people around me; people, things, circumstances, all that comes for teaching, teaching the body to have the true consciousness. It's ... it's marvellous.

(Mother goes within)

It seems that the problem was to create a physical being capable of bearing the Power that wants to manifest - all ordinary bodily consciousnesses are too thin and fragile to withstand the overwhelming Power that is to manifest. And so the body is being accustomed to it. It's as if ... you know, as if it suddenly caught a glimpse of such, such a marvellous horizon ahead, but overwhelmingly marvellous! Then, it is allowed to take only as much of it as it can bear.

Some adaptation is required.

It's quite evident where rest and food are concerned (especially food). It's very strange.... The transition ... right in the middle of the transition.

Will it have enough plasticity? I don't know.

It's a matter of plasticity. To be able to withstand and transmit (*gesture of something flowing through her*), to offer no obstacle to the Power that wants to manifest.

Appearances are only future consequences. That's why.... The appearance is what will change last.

Mother's Agenda, 1.9.71

The human way of being conscious versus the divine way of being conscious...

Everything is a phenomenon of consciousness - everything. Only, it is not a matter of this consciousness, or that one, or that other one, that's not it: it's our way, the human way of being conscious versus the divine way of being conscious. That's all. That's the whole question. And I am thoroughly convinced.

In a word, the world is as it should be at each second.

Yes.

It's we who see it wrongly or feel it wrongly or receive it wrongly.

It's like death, you see. The phenomenon is transitional, but seems to us to have existed forever (it's forever for us because our consciousness is like this [*Mother draws a little square in the air*]), but when you have that divine consciousness, oh!... things become almost instantaneous, you understand. I can't explain it.

Mother's Agenda, 25.12.71

The true consciousness of immortality – life and death change.

I have a feeling I am becoming another person.

No, not just that: I am entering ANOTHER world, another way of being ... which might be called a dangerous way of being (in terms of the ordinary consciousness). As if....

Dangerous, but wonderful - how to express it?

First, the *(body's)* subconscient is in the process of changing, and that is long, arduous and painful ... but marvellous as well. The feeling of ... *(gesture as if standing on a ridge).*

More and more, the body's sensation is that faith alone can save - knowledge is not yet possible, so only faith can save.

But "faith can save" still sounds like an old manner of speaking.... How to phrase it?... The feeling that the relation between what we call "life" and what we call "death" is becoming more and more different - yes, different *(Mother nods her head)*, completely different.

175

Not that death disappears, mind you (death as we see it, as we know it and in relation to life as we know it): that's not it, not it at all. BOTH are changing ... into something we don't yet know, which seems at once extremely dangerous and absolutely marvellous. Dangerous: the least mistake has catastrophic consequences. And marvellous.

It is the consciousness, the true consciousness of immortality - not "immortality" as we understand it, something else. Something else.

Our natural tendency is to want certain things to be true (those we deem favourable) and other things to disappear - but that's not it! It isn't like that. EVERYTHING is different.

Different.

From time to time, for a moment (a brief moment): a marvel. But the very next minute, the feeling of ... a dangerous unknown. There you are. That's how I spend my time.

Mother's Agenda, 7.12.72

Death can be overcome.

(Mother first translates into French the following extract from a letter of Sri Aurobindo:)

"As for immortality, it cannot come if there is attachment to the body, for it is only by living in the immortal part of oneself which is unidentified with the body and bringing down its consciousness and force into the cells that it can come. I speak of course of yogic means.

The scientists now hold that it is (theoretically at least) possible to discover physical means by which death can be overcome, but that would mean only a prolongation of the present consciousness in the present body. Unless there is a change of consciousness and change of functionings it would be a very small gain."

Sri Aurobindo, Letters on Yoga, p.314

176

Mother's experiences with death

It can happen any time at all, I am always ready.

Quite evidently, the adverse forces are not only trying to convince everyone but me too, that this is how it's going to turn out.

But I have as yet had no indications.

I have asked to be forewarned, not for reasons of.... It can happen any time at all, I am always ready. I can do nothing more for the work than what I am doing now, and I haven't a single practical measure to take because I have already taken them all. So that isn't why, but to ... AS MUCH AS POSSIBLE to withdraw from the body all that has been put into it. There is such an accumulation inside it of force, consciousness, power, oh! ... All the cells are impregnated and it would take some time if it all had to be taken out. But I have had no indication of this, neither by night nor by day, neither awake nor in trance - no indication. The indication rather points to all that must be clarified, purified so the physical may keep what it received from that experience (of January 24th, 1961).

From an ordinary standpoint, I believe the situation is dangerous, because ... *(laughing)* the doctor refuses to tell me what the consequences might be. I asked him but he wouldn't tell me, so that's what it must mean! But I really have no indications and ... I hope I won't be told, 'Now you must go.' Only at the very last minute!

Mother's Agenda, 11.2.61

All depends exclusively - exclusively - on ... what the Lord has decided.

But truly speaking, the minute one completely emerges from the ordinary mind, NO EXTERIOR SIGN IS A PROOF,

absolutely none. There is absolutely no standard to go by
- neither splendid good health nor good equilibrium, nor an
almost general disorganization - none of these. All depends
exclusively - exclusively - on ... what the Lord has decided.
Exclusively. Consequently, if one remains very quiet, one is
sure to know what He has decided.

When I am perfectly tranquil, I immediately live in a beatific
joy where questions don't arise – there are no questions! One
asks for nothing – one LIVES! One lives happily, and that's all.
There's no, 'Will it be like this? Will it be like that?' – how
childish! There are no questions, questions don't arise. One is
a beatitude manifesting, that is all.

All the rest is unimportant.

Mother's Agenda, 11.2.61

**So we are after another solution, since death isn't
considered to be a solution. And it's obvious that it is
no solution.**

And curiously, everything comes and presents itself as images
and possibilities; so I say to myself, "But if after a time all
this suddenly stops functioning, what will have been the
use of doing all this work?" And there is always something
- something that comes from a very absolute region -
which makes me feel or understand or grasp the uselessness
of death.

Why am I thus made to feel the uselessness of death?...

God knows, never, not one minute in my life, even when
things were the darkest, the blackest, the most negative, the
most painful, not once did the thought come, "I would like
to die." And ever since I had the experience of psychic
immortality, the immortality of consciousness, that is, in
1902 or 3, or 4 at the latest (sixty years ago now), all fear of
death went away. Now the body's cells have the sense of
their immortality. There was also a time when I almost had
a sort of curiosity about death; it was satisfied by my two
experiences in which, according to the surface illusion, my

178

body was dead, while, within, I had a wonderfully intense life (the first time, it was in the vital, the other time, way up above *(In the vital with Théon, when Mother was looking for the mantra of life and Théon, in a fit of anger, cut the "thread". Way up above, with Sri Aurobindo.)* So that even that curiosity (I can't call it "curiosity"), even that question is no longer asked by the cells. But the possibility does present itself: according to the ordinary outer logic, if this isn't transformed, it must necessarily come to an end. And always, always, I receive the same answer, which isn't an answer with words, but an answer with a knowledge (how can I put it?...), a FACTUAL knowledge: "It's no solution." To say things in quite a banal way, this is the answer: "It's no solution."

So we are after another solution, since death isn't considered to be a solution. And it's obvious that it is no solution.

Yes, it's a failure.

No, it may not be a failure if it's the Lord's Will. It's no longer ours. It's not that we run off, you understand: it's He who decides that it's over.

So the answer comes (not from me, it comes from very far and it's quite ABSOLUTE as a vibration): "It's no solution." It means it isn't, in the present case, considered to be the solution.

There must be another one.

Yes, certainly.

Our imagination is very poor. As for me, I can't imagine how it could happen! I can imagine novels, what I call the pulp novels of spiritual life, but that's nothing, it's childish.

Mother's Agenda, 21.11.64

I am absolutely like a dead person in relation to the earth.

179

Yesterday or the day before, the whole day from morning to evening, something was saying, "I am ... I am or have the consciousness of a dead person on earth." I am putting it into words, but it seemed to say, "This is how the consciousness of a dead person is in relation to the earth and physical things.... I am a dead person living on earth." According to the stand of the consciousness (because the consciousness changes its stand constantly), according to the stand of the consciousness, it was, "This is how the dead are in relation to the earth," then, "I am absolutely like a dead person in relation to the earth," then, "I am the way a dead person lives without any consciousness of the earth," then, "I am quite like a dead person living on earth..." and so on. And I went on speaking, acting, doing as usual.

But it has been like that for a long time.

For a very long time, more than two years, I saw the world like this *(ascending gesture, from one level to a higher level)*, and now I see it like this *(descending gesture)*. I don't know how to explain it because there's nothing mentalized about it, and non-mentalized sensations have a certain haziness that's hard to define. But words and thought were a certain distance away *(gesture around the head)*, like something that watches and appreciates, in other words, that tells what it sees - something around. And today, it has been extremely strong two or three times (I mean that that state dominated the whole consciousness): a sort of impression (or sensation or perception, but it's nothing like all that) of, "I am a dead person living on earth."

How can I explain that?

And then, with vision, for instance, the objective precision is missing *(Mother makes a gesture of not seeing through her eyes)*. I see through and with the consciousness. With hearing, I hear in a totally different way; there is a sort of "discrimination" (it isn't "discernment"), something that chooses in the perception, something that decides (that decides, but not arbitrarily - automatically) what is heard and what isn't heard, what is perceived and what isn't perceived.

It's already there in vision, but it's still stronger with hearing: with certain things, all that's heard is a continuous drone; others are heard very clearly, as clear as crystal; still others are blurred, half heard. With sight, it's the same thing: everything is behind a sort of luminous fog (very luminous, but it's a fog, which means there is no precision), then all at once, a particular thing will be absolutely precise and clear, seen with a most precise vision of detail. The vision is generally the expression of the consciousness in things. That is, everything seems to become more and more subjective, less and less objective.... And they aren't visions that impose themselves on the sight, or noises that impose themselves on the hearing: it's a sort of movement of consciousness that makes certain things perceptible and keeps others as if in a very imprecise background.

The consciousness chooses what it wants to see.

There is a sort of certitude in the body that if, for the space of just a few seconds, I lost contact ("I", meaning the body), if the body lost contact with the Supreme, it would die that very moment. It's only the Supreme that keeps it alive. That's how it is. So naturally, to the ignorant and stupid consciousness of human beings, that's a pitiable condition - and to me, it's the true condition! Because for them, instinctively, spontaneously and in a so to say absolute way, the sign of perfection is the power of life, of ordinary life.... Well, that no longer exists at all - it's completely gone.

Yes, quite a few times, several times, the body did ask the question, "Why don't I feel Your Power and Your Force in me?" And the answer was always a smiling answer (I am putting it into words, but it's wordless), the answer is always: "Patience, patience, you must be READY for that to be."

Mother's Agenda, 9.3.66

181

But death, too, is the result of the taste for drama.

Because what took place is nothing new, it has happened so many times before, but the body's experience was different.... Previously, the consciousness of all the other inner beings was there and would happily counterbalance this idiotic tendency: even the vital, the vital being which also loves grand effects, but provided at least they are great, vast, powerful enough to be on a large scale and save it from being ridiculous; and then, positively above all that, all the other beings, with a smile. But this time, this body was left TO ITSELF, so it would learn. And it has learned.

But death, too, is the result of the taste for drama - what a pretty drama, ugh!

[...]

It went on worsening nicely, till the day (I forget which) when I said with high indignation *(Mother takes on a dramatic tone),* "What is this creation in which..." (I said it in English) "in which living is a suffering, dying is a suffering, everything is a suffering...." *(Mother laughs)* As soon as that was uttered, it was enough. And the consciousness was there, saying, "There is only one remedy, but the world rejects that remedy." Then I was put in the presence of the fact, face to face with it, the thing staring at me - oh, what a pretty drama!

Silence

I wondered whether it was peculiar to the earth and if the other planets and suns weren't in this idiotic situation? ... On an external level it would be interesting to know. But I am nearly sure that death, for instance, is something that belongs exclusively to earth life - death as we FEEL it, as we understand it. Yet animals take part in it, but they don't have man's mental deformation.... The taste for drama is exclusively human, because those animals that live with man catch the malady, while those that don't, don't have it at all.
[...]

For two days the sense of not knowing whether you are alive or dead (but these are words on the surface), of not being very sure of the difference it makes.... And then, the body asking this question: "But everyone has his theory: one says death is like this, another says it's like that, yet another says still something different, but what is our OWN experience like?..." And it was like that *(gesture of hanging between two worlds)*.

Then the body suddenly remembered (that was rather interesting; it's more recent, it was yesterday or the day before), the body suddenly remembered that it had once been brought back to life. It said, "But you knew at that time, you knew since you brought me back to life." *(In Tlemcen with Théon, when in the course of an experience the link with the body was snapped.)* Then I recollected what I used to know (and had stopped knowing because the knowledge was quite incomplete - it was entirely external and lacked the higher knowledge), I recollected the experience, and the two things joined together (the old knowledge and the new). "Now," I said, "this is interesting!"

You know, the story of the "soul leaving the body," what childishness! Because I had that experience, too, of leaving (not the soul! It's entirely independent, always and in everyone), of leaving the psychic being, the individual psychic being.

When I went away from here in 1915, I left my psychic being here deliberately. I left it here, I didn't take it with me. So the body can live without a psychic being (it was rather sick, by the way, but that wasn't the reason - it's again the taste for drama! Oh, always the taste for drama!).

There we are.

So the problem narrows down more and more.... If your most material vital being goes out, it doesn't make you die - it puts you in catalepsy, but it doesn't make you die. What makes you die?...

There are two things that make you die. One (the one that precedes the dramatic human existence) is wear and tear. What does wear and tear come from? From Ignorance, obviously.

Ignorance and incapacity to renew forces; that's how the whole lower life works: it decomposes, recomposes, decomposes again.... But it's only with animality and the beginning of a mental functioning that there arises *(Mother takes on a grandiloquent tone)* "death," as we conceive it. But that is when the vital element that gives life (what we call "life") breaks down. There are innumerable reasons for that, all of which come from the same source. Of course, looking at it as a whole, it is the incapacity to follow the movement of progress: the need to mix everything together again in order to start all over again. But for those who begin to think, that no longer has any reason to exist.

An accident?... An accident to the material combination. But which accident, since the heart can stop and start again? It's a question of how long the accident lasts.

If, for this wear and tear, this deterioration (which comes from the Inconscient and is the result of the RESISTANCE of the Inconscient), if for this we can substitute the aspiration for progress and transformation (not with words - the vibration) ... That experience has been given me several times. Suppose something is quite upset, there is a pain somewhere, something disorganized that no longer works properly; if there is the vision and conception in faith (faith and consecration to the Supreme) that it's deliberate, that the Supreme has allowed it to be (how can I express it? All words are meaningless), has allowed or willed it, or wanted it to be, because to Him it was the best way to transform the thing, to have it make the necessary progress, if the cells that are somewhat disorganized and "sick", as they say, are able to feel this ... then, instantly, it takes a marvellous turn for the better - instantly, in five minutes, ten minutes. I could give concrete, precise examples, with all the details. So that means bringing the two extremes into contact, I might say. And if that can become the normal life of the elements which make up this outer form, then there is no reason why ...

No, there is no need to die, no need whatsoever. There comes a point when death loses all meaning.

And in the small detail, in the little cell or the faint sensation (and when you come to feelings, there is some kind of thing which is the embryo of thought - oh, then ...), you catch the taste for drama. Ah, then everything is explained.

The taste for drama, the need for catastrophe.

That's what was there, pressing and pressing on the earth to bring about all the conditions for a clashing and clangoring grand finale (*Mother shrugs her shoulders*).

And only one remedy: to broaden into eternal peace ... To break limits, become immense.

Long silence

You said just a while ago that your body remembered an earlier death ...

Oh, yes.

But you didn't say what that recollection was.

Yes, everybody knows it: it happened at Tlemcen while I was working with Théon. I had gone out in a wholly material way, the body was in a cataleptic state, and something came, something occurred that cut the link. So the link was cut.

But what was the experience like at that time?

The experience was that ... *(laughing)* impossible to get back in there! But Théon was there (Théon had a bad scare!), and there was at that time the knowledge - a good deal of knowledge! - of the occult. The knowledge was there as well as the will (*Mother makes a gesture of pushing to re-enter the body*), and also an inner faith (but I never used to talk about that), and a concentration. As for him, he was capable, he knew. He was able to "pull". And the body hadn't deteriorated, you see, it wasn't damaged, so it wasn't difficult. It was in a very good condition, but the thread was cut, which means that what gives life had gone out and could not get back in.

I came back in as a result of the power and the will, because ... In fact, simply because I still had something to do on earth.

It happened in 1910, I think.

So it's not because the soul leaves the body, is it?

Oh, that's just words!

The soul may very likely make a resolve, noting that the body is either unworthy or unfit or incapable or unwilling or ... anything, and the soul may decide that the body should die so it may go; but the soul's going isn't what kills the body. There are innumerable people who are without a soul - they have a soul, but their soul isn't in their body - lots of people. And they go on living quite well.

It's more difficult to live without the psychic being, on the other hand. The psychic being, of course, is the clothing - the individualized clothing - between the eternal soul and the transitory body; and *(from life to life)* it grows more formed, individualized, more and more individually conscious. When that leaves the body, the rest generally follows. But I had the experience of doing it deliberately, so I KNOW. One has to know how to do it, but it can be done. My psychic being stayed here with Sri Aurobindo, and I left with my mental, vital and physical beings. It was a ... slightly precarious condition. But as I also kept the contact quite consciously, it could be done.

What people call "death" ... I see loads of people who, to me, are living dead (they are those who are without their psychic being, or even those who have no contact with their soul). But to know that, one must have the inner vision. But what people call "death", that is the decomposition of the cells and dissolution of the form, is when the most material "vital sub-degree", which brings into contact with Life - with vital force, life - goes out. That is how death occurs in animals, for example.

And that vital sub-degree generally goes away when the external organism is unable to continue - when, for instance, it's cut in two or the heart has been removed, or anyway when something quite radical has happened to it! Because some people have met with accidents and had many parts missing, yet they lived on. But even cardiac arrest, as I said, doesn't necessarily mean death, since after stopping, the heart can start up again. Those who have the material knowledge tell you that for a few ... I forget whether a few seconds or a few minutes, the heart can start up again; after that, decomposition sets in. With decomposition it's over, naturally.

So we could correctly say that there are kinds of GRADATIONS in death. Gradations in life and gradations in death: some beings are alive to a greater or lesser degree, or if we want to put it negatively, some beings are dead to a greater or lesser degree. But for those who know, oh, for those who know that this material form can manifest a Supramental light, well, those who don't have the Supramental light in them are already a little dead. That's how it is. So there are gradations. What people have conventionally called "death" is just a purely external phenomenon, because it's something they can't deny - the body going to pieces.

But I have seen people who were supposedly dead (not many in my family because it wasn't the custom to let the children see them, and once I was grown-up there were only very few opportunities), but I have seen a few here. And they weren't all in the same state at all - far from it.

Silence

There was the case of Sri Aurobindo. "He is dead," the doctors decided - he was absolutely alive. Absolutely living. And even after five days, when they put him into ... it was because of (how should I put it?) the pressure of the outside world, and because it was impossible to preserve him. We had to consent. But I cannot say he was dead! He wasn't at all dead, it was perfectly obvious. The body was already

187

beginning to ... (very little, but a little at the end of the fifth day), that is, the skin was losing its colour, but ... *(Mother makes a glorious gesture).*

For the first three days, I remained standing there, near his bed, and in an absolutely ... well, to me, it was absolutely visible - all the organized consciousness that was in his body DELIBERATELY came out of it and into mine. And I not only saw it but felt the FRICTION of its entry.

Then people said, "He is dead" - that's ignorance.
(silence)

All that Supramental power he had attracted into and organized in his body little by little came into me METHODICALLY.

I didn't say anything to anyone because it was nobody's business, nobody's concern. I remained standing there and ... *(gesture showing the forces passing from Sri Aurobindo into Mother's body).*

You know, people revel in high-sounding words and keep talking and talking - they don't even know what they're talking about.

Not very long ago, I saw one or two photographs of someone, then he came to see me. I said, "He is dead, he's a dead man." And I don't mean a dissolution at all (of course not! Since he came in and spoke - he spoke very loudly, thinking himself very alive, in fact): he was dead. So...

Silence

Some time ago, I said that the cells were wondering, "But what is death?" They kept wondering like that. And just yesterday or the day before, because there came a certain state, the Knowledge that constantly comes from above seemed to be saying to them, "But why do you wonder? You had the experience, you know how it is." Then, to the small central consciousness (there is a small central consciousness *(the mind of the cells),* which is now gradually growing and taking shape), this Knowledge said, "Don't you remember? You know how it was." Ah, then all the memory of the experience in all its details came back - they did know.

Mother's Agenda, 14.6.67

The only support is the Divine.

It's absolutely obvious, absolutely indisputable that all this, that is, all the circumstances of life, all that happens, has been willed, decided on, organized. And it's the best possible training for the body. It's to give it three things.

The first is (one more English word) a reliance – that is, it should lean on the Divine ALONE for support, for the source of its strength, its health, its capacity; it means that all material rules and laws are rejected and must cease to have any importance.

That's the body's experience almost every minute.

This first: the only support is the Divine – food, rest, etc, none of those things exist anymore. They no longer exist – in fact, they don't exist, but they no longer exist as a factor of importance.

Then, two things, which seem to be contradictory (in the ordinary consciousness they are), but which in fact are only complementary. A surrender (there's no other word), a total abdication - total, immediate, complete. That is to say, equality and acceptance - not even "acceptance": everything, everything is good, everything is good. Which means that if death were to come tomorrow, it would cause no trouble, and if life must last forever, it causes no trouble - like that, you understand *(perfectly equal and sovereign gesture)*: SPONTANEOUS, spontaneous, effortless acceptance, without reasoning, without ... spontaneous and total, like that *(same gesture)*. That's the second point.

And the third: a tre-men-dous will! Every moment it expresses itself as ... For instance, something is thrown out of gear, it hurts; then, with that background ... it isn't a "background," it's a BASE, a base of equality (equality is still

189

seen from the other side! It's not that, it is ... an adherence, a spontaneous adherence), on that base, there is a tremendous will – tremendous – to be ... WHAT THE DIVINE WILLS, but not with the idea that it might be like this or like that. Well, to express it truly, we should say, "To be divine" – to be divine. That is, to dominate all situations, all wills, all circumstances, like that (*same perfectly equal and sovereign gesture*).

So those three things are simultaneous and constantly present. And all that is going on in the body.

The body (this is becoming interesting) has the same experiences on the heights of the consciousness, the same experiences (Supramental ones, we could say, because, well, there, it's really Supramental) as the vital, the mind and the inner beings had previously.

It's going through the same experiences – the body itself.

That happened the last few nights: it suddenly remembered the time (some twenty years ago, for instance) when those experiences were experiences of the vital, the mind, the psychic being and above. It was the way of being there (*gesture above*), but the body was left out: it was in a different way, in its own way. But now, it's the body: the same experiences, the very same, come back to it like that, and with a certitude and solidity in their base that are incomparable!

There are still, in a subconscious background, bad habits – all the bad habits: defeatism, doubt, pessimism, all that (it's a way of being of that region), but it has gone underground, and when it does come through (more out of habit than out of bad will), when it ... in English I would say *bubbles out,* it gets such a slap!

I clearly see that when this state of will (there is really only one way to put it and it looks like a masquerade, but it's "to be divine," like that, an all-powerful will), when that becomes the normal and spontaneous way of being, then we'll begin to have serious results.

There is still something that watches itself be – which means there is still much that isn't as it should be.

But there are slight oscillations between the old habit of yielding, of being human (with all that it entails), and the other way of being. The other way is vigilant, it's on the alert and says, "No, no! No more of that, no more! The time for that is over." Because, very clearly, that means a slide towards death; the other way is the ascent towards ... we won't yet say "immortality" because that's difficult for this substance, but life at will.

We'll see.

There's a very clear vision, now, very clear and certain, that death is the acceptance of defeat, so ... But everywhere, and for everybody.

Previously, it was an inescapable habit (Mother draws a circle), the inevitable outcome – it's no longer that at all, no longer at all! It's still the memory of a disastrous past.

There.

Mother's Agenda, 10.2.68

It's through this phenomenon of concentration, development and scattering that Matter in its totality evolves.

I have even seen that those cells that have been specially developed and have become conscious of the divine Presence within themselves, when the concentration that gives shape to the body is stopped and the body dissolves (it dissolves little by little), all those conscious cells spread out and enter other combinations in which, through contagion, they awaken the consciousness of the Presence each of them had. So then, it's through this phenomenon of concentration, development and scattering that Matter in its totality evolves, so to speak, and learns through contagion, develops through contagion, experiences through contagion.

But what enters other combinations isn't the cell itself - it's the subtle consciousness of the cells?

Yes, of course! The cell, too, dissolves. It's the CONSCIOUSNESS of the cells that penetrates others.

It's very hard to explain to one who doesn't have the experience.

Mother's Agenda, 3.6.68

The Absolute: absolute Knowledge, absolute Will, absolute Power ... Nothing, nothing can resist...

The cells themselves were saying their effort to be transformed, and there was a Calm.... (How can I explain this...) The body was saying its aspiration and will to prepare itself, and, not asking but striving to be what it should be; all that always with this question (it's not the body that asks it, it's ... the environment, those around - the world, as if the world were asking the question): "Will it continue, or will it have to dissolve?..." The body is like this *(gesture of abandon, hands open upward)*, it says, "What You will, Lord." But then, it knows the question is decided, and One doesn't want to tell it - it accepts. It doesn't lose patience, it accepts, it says, "Very well, it will be as You will." But That which knows and That which doesn't answer is ... something that can't be expressed. It is ... yes, I think the only word that can describe the sensation it gives is "an Absolute" - an Absolute. Absolute. That's the sensation: of being in the presence of the Absolute. The Absolute: absolute Knowledge, absolute Will, absolute Power ... Nothing, nothing can resist. And then this Absolute (there's this sensation, concrete) is so merciful! But if we compare it with all that we regard as goodness, mercy ... ugh! that's nothing at all. It's THE Mercy with the absolute power and ... it's not Wisdom, not Knowledge, it's ... It has nothing to do with our process. And That is everywhere, it's everywhere. It's the body's experience. And to That it has given itself entirely, totally, without asking anything – anything. A single aspiration *(same gesture, hands open upward)*, "To be capable of being That, what That wills, of serving That" – not even "serving," of BEING That.

192

But that state, which lasted for several hours ... never had this body, in the ninety-one years it's been on earth, felt such happiness: freedom, absolute power, and no limits *(gesture here and there and everywhere)*, no limits, no impossibilities, nothing. It was ... all other bodies were itself. There was no difference, it was only a play of the consciousness ... *(gesture like a great Rhythm)* moving about.

So there.

Apart from that, all the rest is as usual.

Mother's Agenda, 15.2.69

But now the body has learned to be ab-so-lute-ly indifferent to those reactions – absolutely.

The body is aware that That, this Consciousness, knows full well whether it will continue or not. It has never been told anything, and it knows (it has felt the two things equally, as equal certitudes, and with equal acceptance), it knows this is the most favourable condition for the work, so it doesn't ask anything. There are worries around (of all kinds), from an anguish at the idea that it could happen (all around, like that) to *(laughing)* a haste for the end to come! (That also happens.) But now the body has learned to be ab-so-lute-ly indifferent to those reactions - absolutely. It smiles. It smiles with this benevolent Smile *(of the superman consciousness)*, it has the same smile. And it sees, it knows, it senses where that *(the worry or the "haste")* comes from, it's thoroughly conscious. After all, it's very amusing! There's a whole gamut, a whole scale, from fear (a semi-conscious, blind fear) to ... *(Mother laughs)* an impatient desire! "Free at last! Free at last to do all the foolish things I want to do!..." It seems there aren't many, but there are some. The two opposites of blind Ignorance coming together. The body has become very conscious: it's very sensitive to what comes from people. It didn't have that before, but now it senses.

193

It's supported, helped: this superman consciousness that has come helps it a lot, it's through it that the body feels, and that helps it a lot. Sometimes, when someone comes in, along with him (him or her or them) comes a slight acute uneasiness; if the body had felt that before knowing, it would have been painful, but now it can smile and wait to discover why it's like that *(Mother gestures as if to trace the vibration that caused the uneasiness)*. With others, on the contrary, the atmosphere is immediately filled with the presence of this Consciousness (that's new, and very interesting), so then the body feels fine – it feels fine, rested.

There were lots and lots of things with a question mark before: "Why is it like this?" Now it knows, it's beginning to know why – that's amusing. And it has begun to know why since it completely abdicated and lost any eagerness either to go on or to stop (either one or the other); it's like this *(gesture of surrender)*: "What You will, Lord; as long as You want me to be like this, I'll be like this; when or if You want me not to be, I won't be" – it's completely, absolutely unimportant.

Mother's Agenda, 19.2.69

There are minutes when the body feels it has escaped that law of death.

Why? Why that habit of suddenly coming apart, why? ... Of course, it's not something new that came with man, because it was the same thing with all that preceded him: it would take form, dissolve - take form, live, grow, and dissolve - everything: plants and ... The mineral kingdom was more stable by virtue of its unconsciousness(!), but all the rest was like that, constantly taking form, losing form, taking form and losing form again .... Then man made a fuss about it, of course, and a drama. He dramatized it, and because he dramatized it he endeavours ... not to get out of it, but to adjust himself - to understand and adjust himself. And when you are in a certain consciousness, it simply looks like foolishness, nothing else. But why? ... Is the human body incapable of...? It's not even that, I can't even say that. There are minutes (minutes, it doesn't last), minutes when the body feels it has escaped that law *(of death)*. But it doesn't last; it's for one minute, then it passes and things are back as they were. But the body consciousness is beginning to wonder why it's like that: Why, why isn't there ... a growth in light and in consciousness, an indefinite growth? Why? The body itself wonders why. Also, it's constantly assailed by all the... well, the general corruption; and once in a while - once in a while - a flash of light, lasting ... a few seconds: all of a sudden, something else. Something else and ... a wonderful consciousness, and then the old routine goes on.

Mother's Agenda, 10.5.69

I don't know if I am alive, I don't know if I am dead.

If you asked the body, it would say, "I don't know if I am alive, I don't know if I am dead." Because that's really how it is. For a few minutes it absolutely has the feeling of being dead; at other times, it has the feeling of being alive. The body is like that. And it feels that exclusively depends on ... whether the Truth is perceived or not.

Silence

What does it depend on?...

Silence

According to what others say or write or experience, I have seen that what the vast majority of humanity fears the most is this perception of the Falsehood of it all, and all that leads to it. I know people (they've written to me) who just these last few days have had terrible frights, because all of a sudden they were forcibly seized, something was beginning to touch them: the perception of the unreality of life. So that shows the

195

immensity of the path still ahead. Which means that any hope of a solution near at hand seems childish. Unless ... things take place differently.

If things must follow the movement they've followed till now ... How many centuries and centuries and centuries there have been... So the superman would only be one more stage, and after him there would be many other things.

Mother's Agenda, 31.5.69

The only, only way out that is effective is in fact self-abandon, surrender.

Looking at what happens from one day to the next, the body's experience is like this... In a certain way, at certain times, it's in the consciousness of Immortality, and then, out of influence (also out of habit now and then), it falls back into the consciousness of mortality, and that's really... For it now, as soon as it falls back into the consciousness of mortality, there's a dreadful anguish; it's only when it emerges from that, when it enters the true consciousness, that it passes. I understand why some people, yogis, spoke of the unreality of the world, because, for the consciousness of Immortality, the consciousness of mortality is an unreal absurdity. And it's like this *(Mother slips the fingers of one hand between the fingers of the other, showing an alternation between the two consciousnesses)*. So now it's like this, now it's like that. And the other state, the state of Immortality, is immutably peaceful, tranquil, with ... like lightning-fast waves, so rapid that they seem still. It's like this: complete motionlessness (apparently) within a tremendous Movement. But then, as soon as the other state comes, it's all the ordinary notions that come back, that is to say ... really in its present state, that gives it the anguish and suffering of a falsehood. But it's still like this *(same to-and-fro gesture)*....

The only, only way out that is effective is in fact self-abandon, surrender. It's not expressed in words or an idea or anything, but it's a state, a state of vibration, in which ONLY the Divine Vibration has value. Then - then things get back in order.

But all that, the moment you talk about it...

But note that it's constant: it happens in the night, it happens in the morning (mornings are generally very difficult), and then there are other times when... *(immense, even gesture, with a smile)* there are no more problems - all problems are over: no more problems, no more difficulties, nothing anymore.

Silence

There's a background (it's mostly that), a background of unconscious Negation which is still behind everything, but everything; it's still there everywhere: you eat or breathe - you receive that Negation.... For everything to be transformed, it's still a colossal work. But when you are on the "other side", as we might call it (it's not "sides"), in the other state, it seems so natural that you wonder why things aren't like that, why they seem so difficult. And then, as soon as you're back to this other side, it's... *(Mother takes her head in her hands)* ... The mixture is still there, undeniably.

Truly, the ordinary state, the old state, is consciously (meaning it's a conscious perception), it's death and suffering. And then in the other state, death and suffering appear to be absolutely unreal - there you are.

Mother's Agenda, 18.10.69

The body consciousness was the consciousness of a dying body.

It was a rather peculiar night... An old friend of Amrita's died in the night: Ganeshan. I didn't know. And it was...

How can I really explain? ... The body, the body consciousness was the consciousness of a dying body, and at the same time with the perfect knowledge that it wasn't dying.

197

But it was the consciousness of a dying body, with all the anguish, all the suffering, all those things, but there was the knowledge that it wasn't this (*Mother points to her own body*) that was dying. And it lasted a long time: it lasted all night – he died very early this morning. Afterwards, I knew (only a few hours afterwards, when I was told that he had left), then I understood...

That man was very ardent in his devotion and he had long known that he was going to die; his sons had proposed to take him away for treatment – he said, "No, I want to die at the Ashram, I don't want to leave the atmosphere..." And I understand why, because... you see, the consciousness was there helping him all along, he instantly had the reaction this body *(Mother's)* would have, you understand? Which means he died in particularly favourable conditions, my body was like this *(gesture of surrender)* and saying, "All right, Lord, it's as You will, I am quite ready." At the same time, it perfectly had the knowledge: "But you aren't dying!..." Like that.

But that's how it was, it said, "Very well, if You have decided. You have decided...." And it knew. I can't say it spent a good night, no! But the consciousness was very, very, very conscious, oh!...

So then, when it (the body) was told in the morning that that man had left *(laughing)*, it laughed, it said, "Oh, so that's what it was!..."

But it was interesting. And it's after this (I forget at what time, but probably when it felt it was over or was going to be over – at any rate the intensity of the "operation" was past) that I immediately had that vision: the body entered its usual rest, and the next thing, I was in that car – that world car driven by Sri Aurobindo... And so, so TRULY clear, living, real – extraordinary!

Mother's Agenda, 28.1.70

198

Basically, what still has the illusion of being something separate must dissolve.

The other day I told you that the body had had the experience of dying without dying, and it was useful in that the body said, "Well...it's all right."

Accept without.... (what's the word?) without effort – ADHERE. Then it's over: The entire old illusion of disappearing with the body's dissolution, it's a long time since it went away, of course, and now the body itself is quite convinced that even if it were scattered like that *(in 'death'),* that would widen its field of consciousness... I don't even know how to explain because for the consciousness, this sense of the personal and the need of the personal has vanished.

I clearly see, the body clearly realizes that it's only its own resistance – its resistance to the Truth – that makes it possible for it to suffer. Wherever there is complete adherence, suffering disappears instantly.

Silence

But it's the same thing for countries and nations: it's the same change of authority. Instead of personal authorities, there will be a divine authority, and the same change of authority causes the unspeakable chaos we live in – because of the resistance.

Long silence

The nearer a part of the being (any part) draws to the moment of the transition, that is, the more ready it is for that transition, the more sensitive it becomes. And then, when you reach the point where you can go beyond the stage of problems and see with the universal vision, problems take on, to the personal sensitiveness, a most intense acuteness. I had noticed it before, and now it's recurring for the body. It's acquiring a ... terrifying sensitiveness, you understand. People who don't know why things are like that really get terrified.... The possibility of discomfort, of... It's the same thing with problems. Only, for those who KNOW and who have understood, it's the opportunity of making the last progress, of doing this (*Mother opens her hands upward*).

Basically, what still has the illusion of being something separate must dissolve. It must say to itself, "It's not my business, I don't exist." That's the best attitude it can take. Then ... it goes into the great Universal Rhythm.

Mother's Agenda, 31.1.70

Well, if it's not possible in your body, how will it be possible in other bodies?

I don't like to speak of myself. Only... (that's something I don't know: whether my body will be preserved or not – I have no idea and it doesn't interest me), it seems to me that it could be useful only if this body is gone.

Oh, listen!

Silence

Not gone – changed.

Oh, changed – is it possible?

Well, if it's not possible in your body, how will it be possible in other bodies?

No, I don't know. For man, it seems established that his progress is made from birth to birth, with very fleeting intermediary births, forms that aren't perpetuated. So it may be that some people, with a body somewhat... (what shall I say?) developed or advanced, could now have children who would themselves have... like this (*snowballing gesture*), and then those intermediary stages would disappear.

Mother's Agenda, 25.3.70

200

I see that "something" as a person watching over my body and over circumstances...

And these last few days, I've had the impression, or something like a perception, an impression of an AWESOME Power! The Power that would seem capable of bringing a dead man back to life, you know. An awesome Power that uses this *(body)* without conscious identification, but quite, quite naturally, without... as if there were no resistance. It's a natural state, and it's neither this nor that nor that, it's... it's EVERYTHING *(gesture showing an immense movement)* which... which acts according to circumstances.

Usually I don't say anything (it's the first time I've said that), because there is still a sort of memory of what was (in the past), something remaining conscious that if those things are said quite simply as they are, then ... the impression people would get ... I don't know. The body doesn't care, but something is watchful – I see that "something" as a person (whom I don't know, besides) watching over my body and over circumstances, and stopping me from doing certain things ... so there may be no catastrophes.

It's an impersonal person, I don't know; there's no personal relationship with it, but it's someone whose responsibility is to see to this body's well-being, and especially to its relations with others, because the body has reached the point where ... it really couldn't care less.

Mother's Agenda, 22.4.70

The presence of the Grace is an absolutely marvellous thing!

But the presence of the Grace is an absolutely marvellous thing! Because as I see things, the experience as it is... if I were not given at the same time the true meaning of what's taking place, it would be endless agony – it's the old way of being which is dying.

201

Naturally, there is the whole yogic preparation, but the body is... you know, it's a constant miracle! People couldn't bear it for more than a few minutes, and it goes on and on and on...

It began exactly on the day of darshan.

Once or twice, the body was offered to go back to the previous condition – it refused. It said, "No, it's EITHER this, or else leaving."

That's why it's going on...

Mother's Agenda, 29.4.70

Before he left, he said no. "No, I shall return when it can be done in a Supramental body."

As for me I ... this body does what it can. It can't do much. It tries ... it tries not to create any resistance. From time to time - from time to time - there's something, a marvel, which lasts for a few seconds. But it's... *(Mother nods her head)*. Either we have to manage to make this body more plastic so it can be transformed, or else it will be for another life.

Although I must say that ... Sri Aurobindo said to me, "Oh, to have to begin all that over again, the whole childhood and all that unconsciousness - no!" Before he left, he said no. "No, I shall return when it can be done in a Supramental body." *(This is what Mother wrote to Sujata's father, Prithwi Singh, in 1953 about the passing away of Sri Aurobindo,)* "At 1:26 in the morning, when I was in his room, he was steadily coming out of his body into mine; it was so much that I felt a physical friction in the cells of my body; with it a great power entered into me and I felt capable of resuscitating him. But when I told him, he said, 'No, it is purposely that I have left my body, I will not come back into it, I will return in a new body, the first body built in the Supramental way.'" "But," *Mother added,* "he did not tell me the time when he would return."

But there have to be bodies capable of lasting at will. He said, "The intermediate stage will be duration of life at will." And I have the feeling that that is possible. Provided ... the body itself thinks only of one thing - transformation. When it is like this *(quiet, concentrated),* then.... I can spend hours - hours without moving - in a kind of receptive contemplation, and it seems like a second.

The sense of time is really curious. You see, there is a certain receptive contemplation, and there *(gesture of being suspended in a smile)* ... time simply ceases to exist.

I sense.... I sense I am on the threshold of a great Secret ... but *(Mother nods her head)* ... not mental - not in thoughts. It's ... "something."

Mother's Agenda, 4.9.71

It's really a period of transition for the body.

The body is realizing, becoming conscious of what in it prevents it from being immortal, and at the same time of what can be immortal in it. It has had moments of agony as never before in its whole life - in connection with death, which has never happened before. And it has understood that its very constitution was causing this, and what it had to change. I am ... as though on the threshold of an extraordinary discovery, but....

Silence

I could put it this way: the why of death has become clear, and the how of immortality is ... *(silence)....* You know, it's a curious thing, the feeling that there is something *(Mother feels with her fingertips)* TO TOUCH.

Mother's Agenda, 8.9.71

203

We are in full transition:

We are in full transition: it is no longer this, it is not yet that.
And the concentration of force is greater and greater.

Silence

A strange experience. It's a strange experience. The body feels
it no longer belongs to the old way of being, but it knows that
it is not yet in the new one and that it is.... It is no longer mortal
and it is not yet immortal. It's quite strange. Very strange.
And sometimes I go from the most dreadful discomfort to ...
a marvel - it's strange. An unutterable bliss. It's no longer this,
and it's not yet that. Well. Bizarre *(Mother nods her head)*.

Silence

There is a sort of promise of an overwhelming Power, and
at the same time signs of such weakness - not weakness:
disorganization. Disorganization, and at the same time the
sense of an overwhelming Power. So the two are like this
(gesture of being in a precarious balance). It's a disorganization
in the sense that if I don't pay attention, I can't eat, for
instance. I have to pay attention, I have to be concentrated all
the time, concentrated in order to do things. Sometimes, not a
word in my head, nothing; sometimes I see and know what is
happening everywhere. It's like this *(same gesture as on a ridge)*.
   I have to be careful when I am with people, otherwise they
would think I am going crazy! *(laughter)*
   It's really peculiar. A sort of total impotence and an
overwhelming power side by side. And the results of the
overwhelming power are sometimes visible in people here and
there: all of a sudden, miraculous things happen. But at the
same time ... sometimes I can't even eat. It's strange. *(Mother
laughs.)*

Mother's Agenda, 18.9.71

204

We need to find the plasticity of matter – so that matter can progress forever.

I have a very strong feeling I have caught the true thing, as if I held (*Mother clenches her fist*) the tail of the true thing. And it explains everything – absolutely everything. And it cancels nothing.

(Mother goes within for a long time)

You have nothing to tell me?

So I shouldn't worry?

No. No, no! If you knew how marvellous it is! Absolutely all the problems have been solved all at once. Only, I can't talk about it.

Don't worry.

It's a hundred times more marvellous than we can possibly imagine.

The question is to know if this (the body) will be able to follow.... To follow, it not only has to last, but it has to acquire a new strength and a new life. That I don't know. In any case, it doesn't matter - the consciousness is clear, and the consciousness is not subject to this *(Mother points to her body)*. If it can be used, so much the better, if not.... There are still things to be found.

Oh, many things to be found! The old routine is over.

It's over.

We need to find the plasticity of matter - so that matter can progress for ever. That's it.

How much time will it take? I don't know. How many experiences will it take? I don't know. But now the direction is clear. The direction is clear.

Mother's Agenda, 30.10.71

Only some kind of violent death, an "accident" could stop the transformation.

We're still in the period of struggle.

Now, the body has the conviction that only death can stop its transformation. So it's impossible. Only some kind of violent death, an "accident" (well...) could stop the transformation, otherwise the work is being done regularly, regularly (*gesture of irresistible advance*). It's like that, the body is convinced of it now, that only violence could stop it - but then if that happens, it's certainly because it had to happen, you see, for some reason ... which it has no desire to know, it doesn't care a button. But otherwise, as long as it's here, it knows that the work will go on and on and on ... in spite of everything. That's it.

Mother's Agenda, 4.12.71

... or else it may be that the body knows it is going to leave.

There's a great need to file, to put things in order.... Perhaps it's simply the Force pressing down, that wants everything to be in order (I think that's what it is) ... or else it may be that the body knows it is going to leave.

No, no! No, no, no - that is not possible!

(*Laughing*) No, of course not!

It does feel a process of transformation taking place. But sometimes it feels it's impossible - it's impossible, you simply can't go on existing like this - but then, just at the last minute, something comes, and then it's ... it's a Harmony totally unknown to this physical world. A Harmony - the physical world seems appalling in comparison. But that doesn't last.

(Mother touches her chest, she is always short of breath when she speaks)

I am finding it more and more difficult to speak.

But my perceptions are clearer and clearer *(Mother draws a sort of picture in front of her)*, clear, luminous. My perceptions are getting clearer and clearer, more and more luminous - vaster and vaster.

It's really like a new world that wants to manifest itself.

In silence, I am comfortable.

(Mother goes into contemplation. After a few moments, a blissful smile spreads over her face.)

Mother's Agenda, 22.1.72

It felt as if enfolded ... like a baby carried in the arms of the Divine...

Two or three days ago (I don't remember when), something was pressing on my heart - and it hurt. It hurt, it was the 24th. I really had the feeling that ... the body had the feeling it was the end. But then immediately, it felt as if enfolded ... like a baby carried in the arms of the Divine. The exact sensation, you know, as if I were a baby being carried in the arms of the Divine. And after some time (a long time), when the body was exclusively in the Presence, it went away. The body didn't even ask for the pain to go; it just left. It took a little while, but it left.

I haven't told anyone. I thought ... I thought the end had come. It was just after lunch....

Absolutely, but absolutely the sensation of being a baby nestling *(gesture)* in the Divine's arms. Extraordinary!

Silence

You see, for a time it's like this: "What You will, what You will...." And then this too falls silent and ... *(Mother opens*

207

her hands upwards in a gesture of offering and immobile contemplation).

Mother's Agenda, 26.2.72

Then if the work must be done, if Auroville must be built, not only do I have to remain in my body but the body must become strong.

As for me, the power of consciousness goes on increasing; for the time being - I repeat, for the time being - the physical power is reduced to almost nought. I am forced to stay here, minding nothing, and make shift with seeing people. So I need some persons to do the practical work I used to do before and can no longer do ... *(Mother is short of breath).* I can't speak with the same strength as before - the physical is undergoing a transformation, you know. Sri Aurobindo himself had said - and rightly so - he said (because one of us had to go, and I offered to go), "No, your body is capable of enduring it, it has the strength to undergo transformation." It's not easy. I can assure you, it's not easy. Yet my body is good-willed, it is really good-willed. But for the moment it is in the process of ... well, it is no longer quite on this side but not yet on the other. The transition isn't easy. So I am stuck here, like an old woman, incapable of doing any work.

If I can hold on - if only I can hold on - at one hundred things will be better. That I know. I am absolutely convinced there will be a renewal of energy. But I have to hold on.... That's all.

Silence

So for the moment, we lack money. We lack money because money is being scattered. People no longer know where to give, so they stop giving: "Should I give here, should I give there, should I...?" They don't give anything anymore.

I can see, I have truly the occasion to see that if I left, I have nobody here, it would be our destruction.

(R.) Oh, complete collapse - nothing!

Then if the work must be done, if Auroville must be built, not only do I have to remain in my body but the body must become strong.

I know. I know that. All depends on what the Divine Will is - He doesn't tell me! When I ask Him, I have the impression ... (once or twice, in moments of difficulty, I have put the question regarding this body), and then *(laughing)* I seem to see a smile, you know, a smile as big as the world, but no answer.

I can still see that smile: "Don't try to know, it is not yet time."

The clock strikes...

If we knew how to remain always in the true consciousness, there would be ... a smile. But we have a tendency to become tragic. It's our weakness.

It is our limitations that make a drama. We are too small - too small and too shortsighted. But ... the Consciousness knows - it knows.

Mother's Agenda, 10.3.72

To prepare for immortality, the consciousness of the body must first become one with the Eternal Consciousness.

Mother's Agenda, 17.3.72

All the old methods are obsolete, but the new ones aren't yet established.

Constantly, but constantly, I have things I would like you to know, but I don't have a chance to tell them. The ordinary memory is all gone, do you know, so if it comes, it comes; if it doesn't come ... it's just lost.

Really ... fantastic things.

As if I were walking on a very thin and narrow line: on one side, imbecility, and on the other genius! That's how I progress *(gesture of standing on a ridge)*.

What does it depend on? I have no idea.

All the old methods are obsolete, but the new ones aren't yet established. Although sometimes, they come all of a sudden: for a few minutes, there's a dazzling flood of light ... something marvellous, the feeling of a power over the entire world. And the next minute, all gone.

Night and day, like that.

Sometimes, for no apparent reason, I am in such a horrible discomfort, I feel it must lead to death, but then ... something says, "Don't mind," as though Sri Aurobindo were watching over me - don't mind, don't mind.... So I ... *(Mother opens her hands)*. And after a little while: gone, it's inexplicably gone.

I can't eat anymore - oh, it's so difficult! So difficult. Eating is really the most difficult of all.... I am not really disgusted by food, nothing of the sort, but I just can't put it in my mouth. I can still drink ... for the moment.

There's nothing there, nothing *(pointing to her forehead)*, it's empty, empty, thoroughly empty.... And when I remain like this....

Mother's Agenda, 3.6.72

As if to demonstrate that you have to go through death in order to conquer death.

210

Nothing. I feel the ... churning one is put through.

Oh!...

Sometimes it feels as if something were ... raging ferociously.

Yes, exactly. As if to demonstrate that you have to go through death in order to conquer death.

Exactly. And just as you are about to cross the threshold, suddenly it's all righted.

I thought I was the only one experiencing that, and I was happy to do it for everybody, but evidently some people feel it also - you feel it.

Oh, do I! Dash it all, it's ... I feel something ferociously raging.

Yes, that's right, quite. And it shows there's a sort of ... difference - a mere difference of attitude; a difference of attitude: the body can either fall apart or be transformed. And it's ... almost the same procedure; only the attitude is different. If you have absolute trust in the Divine and feel to what point the Divine is everywhere and in everything, if you want to depend only on the Divine, belong only to the Divine, then it's perfect. But the least conflict ... and it's like the gates of death suddenly yawning.

Mother's Agenda, 29.7.72

My body was seized by the horror of death.

And then - oh, I haven't told you: yesterday or the day before, I don't remember, all of a sudden, for two or three minutes, my body was seized by the horror of death - the idea of being put like this *(gesture of being tossed into a hole)* in a tomb was so horrifying! Horrifying.... I couldn't have stood that

211

more than a few minutes. It was HORRIFYING. Not because I was buried alive, but because my body was conscious. It was considered "dead" by everybody for the heart had stopped beating - yet the body was conscious.

Silence

That ... that ... that was a horrible experience.... I was displaying all the signs of "death", you know, the heart wasn't working, nothing was working - but I was conscious. The body was conscious.

Silence

We must ... we must warn people at least not to rush to... *(gesture into a hole).*

Mother's Agenda, 10.1.73

Om Namo Bhagavate

212